ALAN HOVHANESS

Artik

Opus 78a

for Horn and Piano

EDITION PETERS

LEIPZIG · LONDON · NEW YORK

Artik, in reference to a seventh-century octagonal church with central dome and four semi-domes.

Duration: 15 minutes

to Carlo and Aghvani Uomini

A R T I K
Concerto for Horn and String Orchestra

1. Alleluia

ALAN HOVHANESS
Op. 78ª

*Solo part for horn printed in F.

Edition Peters 6487A

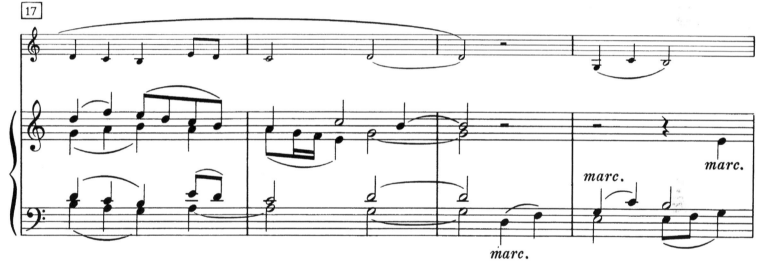

4

2. Ballata

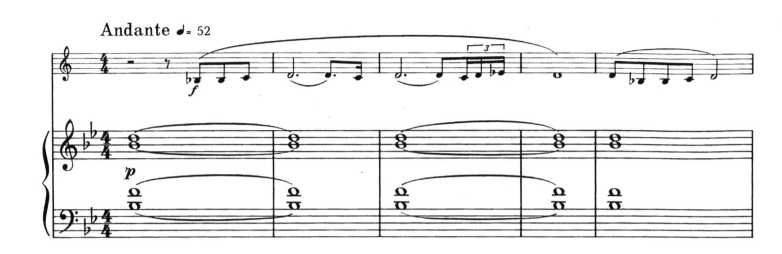

3. Laude

Andante ♩= ca. 66

repeat continuously up to measure 22

5

continue repeating

10

continue repeating

4. Canzona

To a Mountain Range

5. Processional

6. Canon

Allegro ♩ = 132

ad lib. for a second player, may be omitted

pizz.

p sempre staccato

7

pizz.
sempre staccato

12

7. Aria

8. Intonazione

Senza misura

pizz.

repeat continuously in a *pp* murmur up to measure 2

continue repeating

continue repeating

Andante ♩ = 80

To my sister Val who sadly died while I was writing this book.
'We have to do good things…'

And to Amy and Pearl with love.

GHOST
TOWN

A Liverpool Shadowplay

JEFF YOUNG

LITTLE TOLLER

Published by *Little Toller Books* in 2020
FORD, PINEAPPLE LANE, DORSET

Typeset in Garamond by Little Toller Books

Printed in Cornwall by TJ International

All papers used by Little Toller Books are natural, recyclable products made from wood grown in sustainable, well-managed forests

A catalogue record for this book is available from the British Library

ISBN 978-1-908213-78-5

Contents

I am making these arrangements into meaning
to re-inhabit after twenty years some places of
myself – backyards full of ships and cranes,
of hard-knock, talk and death – not just
to mouth at ghosts, unless there's welcoming
in such a courtesy; not merely exorcise:
I'd like to talk at this late stage on equal terms,
Declare a kind of coming of age
To those who have implanted death in me.

Matt Simpson, 'Making Arrangements' from *Elegy for the Galosherman*

.

Gutted Arcades

My mother liked to trespass – she didn't call it trespassing, she called it *having a nose*. We'd have a look round the Corn Exchange or go up the back stairs of an insurance building, slip into the Oriel Chambers and sort of just … breathe. We were breathing in Victorian dust and the pipe smoke of Dickensian ledger clerks; drinking in shadows and gloom and beams of light. We'd stand on fire escapes and gaze across the rooftops. I was short-trousered and eight years old and I was madly in love – with a city.

We used to watch the Watchers, the old men standing at demolition sites. Flat caps, raincoats, smokers coughing and spitting. They were mute witnesses to death, and their grief at the end-days of vanished places that meant so much was palpable. I'd watch them with my mother, who was teaching me the city: it was a living thing that needed our protection and love and the way to do this was to walk its sandstone pavements and just drink it all in. Memorise it.

The city was a collage of thrilling dissonance – Victorian splendour, a Lancashire Chicago, May Blitz bomb sites next to collapsing slums and Viennese-style tenements, bang next to the 1960s science-fiction eyesore of the shopping precinct, the banal Futuropolis of some deranged city planner.

We'd walk for hours through a Liverpool seemingly ripped,

torn and riveted together again, a bricolaged city of back-alley labyrinths, cigarette kiosks, strange arcades and collapsing fruit warehouses; of dusty bookshops, oyster bars and sooty railway stations. But most of all, I remember the cinema queues in the rain on Lime Street, just like the black-umbrella queue in *Distant Voices, Still Lives* – it was a city always more beautiful in the rain.

This city is my muse; its unruliness and awkwardness, its rebellious spirit, its ugliness and beauty filter into the stories I write and make the work wayward and disruptive. I have written characters inspired by the particular atmospheres of certain back alleys and ruined buildings. I have tried to imbue a story with the melancholy beauty of Liverpool's psychedelic sunsets. I had the feeling – still have the feeling – that the city was a living novel and we were walking through its pages. When I was a child it was a pop-up book. When I was older it was Dickensian, or a sprawling Scouse *Ulysses*, full of mystery and gassing and mad characters and adventure. My mother and I were characters in a book being written by some unseen author. Each walk was a chapter, each building was a paragraph, and the spaces in between the words were alleyways and streets. The margins were the river and sky and the pages were alive with the thronging crowd. My hand in my mother's hand, we slipped through the great adventure. When I read this city-book now, its pages come alive with images that shimmer and loom … there's the old man wrestling with a conger eel on the ferry-landing stage, and there's me seesawing on a gangplank, with my Billy Fury quiff.

When I was seventeen I picked up a copy of Malcolm Lowry's *Ultramarine* in a bookshop in Exchange Station – a station used by Lowry, en route to Norway in 1931 – and I discovered that Lowry had been a haunter of Liverpool's streets and cinemas, too. He knew the places my mother knew, he rode the Mersey ferry in the rain as we did, went to the same theatres and picture houses. He describes his hero, his alter-ego, Dana Hilliot:

His whole being was drowning in memories, the smells of
Birkenhead and of Liverpool were again heavily about him, there
was a coarse glitter in the cinema fronts, children stared at him
strangely from the porches of public houses. Janet would be
waiting for him at the Crosville bus stop ... while silver straws
of rain gently pattered on the green roof ... 'Where shall we go?
The Hippodrome or the Argyle? ... I've heard there's a good show
on at the Scala.'

When I read this in 1975, I got that short-circuit feeling I
get when a book makes a direct connection with my own life.
*Malcolm Lowry went to the Scala, where I went to Saturday matinees!
Malcolm Lowry rode Crosville buses!* The same ones we took home
from Skelhorne Street. He even mentioned Great Homer Street,
where my dad had a stall selling junk at the indoor rag market.
He later writes:

At half-past seven, by the clock on the Liver Buildings, he returns
on the ferry from Liverpool ... he smokes his pipe in silence ...
Outside it has started to rain again, a colourless dusty rain ...
Liverpool sweeps away from him in a great arc. Through the
rain-scarred windows he watches Liverpool become rain ...

If I'd always felt the city was a novel, here was proof. Malcolm
Lowry rides the Mersey Ferry, the same *Royal Daffodil* we'd take
across the river to Seacombe! I remember the excitement of sailing
on that very boat, watching as we surged home towards Liverpool
and waiting for my favourite moment, when the boat buffered
up against the enormous tractor tyres hanging off the landing
stage. And the trips on the old New Brighton ferry, often with my
grandfather, and the walks along the promenade watching the teddy
boys flirt with girls clustered around the gallopers and waltzers.

The Pier Head was the most exotic place in the city and my
memories of those visits are almost hallucinatory. Ships from all
over the world docked here. Timber piers splintered and collapsed
into mud-stained waters. Bookies runners and pickpockets

loitered by cigarette machines, spitting on the pavement, eyeing up the prostitutes. It was like a Liverpool version of the carnival in Lowry's *Under the Volcano*, an assembly of misfits and magic men in the wild hullabaloo of the Mersey. Professor Codman would be there with his wooden-headed puppets, and there was a tramp we called Old Man River, always looking out to sea and whom I used to dream was the source of the Mersey, the river pouring out of him and flowing all the way to New York.

Everyone who ever felt like a stray dog came down to the Pier Head on Sundays and the presiding spirit of anarchy in this place was Hughie Smith, Liverpool's Harry Houdini, a man wrapped in chains and tied in a potato sack, a writhing, struggling genius in a vest. I was in awe of him as he thrashed around on the ground like a sack of cats, eventually emerging from captivity, taking a bow to the crowd as the bottler went around the gathering with a hat, collecting sixpences and threepenny bits. Sometimes he would invite people in the crowd to pick up a sledgehammer and smash a concrete slab resting on his chest. One time I saw him being hanged with a rope noose, then carried to Yates's Wine Lodge, where he was revived with a glass of Aussie white. He was a one-man carnival, exotic and unsettling. No one ever explained to me why a man might let another man padlock him up in chains and tie him in a potato sack; he was just accepted as one of Liverpool's unruly characters. In the mad circus parade of the city, Hughie could have been a character dreamed up by Lowry.

Ultramarine is the book where Lowry keeps being pulled back to Liverpool – back *into* Liverpool. As he says in his poem 'Trinity', 'Imprisoned in a Liverpool of self / I haunt the gutted arcades of the past.' He can't resist the pull, he keeps dropping Liverpool rain onto the novel's pages, keeps sauntering down Paradise Street on his way to a memory of a date in a long-dead cinema, and taking that storm-battered ride across the river on the *Daffodil*.

Liverpool night and weather seeps out of its pages and into the reader's dreams; luminous visions of the city, brief glimpses of heartache and loneliness, lit up by department-store windows, street lights and shipyard workers' lanterns. It's as if the further away from Liverpool he travels, the more the city haunts him; he is infected with glimmering ghost-images, perhaps the visions that wake him from delirious sleep with a jolt. He strolls 'slowly in the direction of Egremont Ferry, along the desolate promenade, and past soaking walls where sodden advertisements are clinging like wet rags'. New Brighton beach is black, the Mersey is viscous, and Lowry wakes, seasick drunk, as if he is waking in the Mersey mud, and furiously inks the memory onto the page before it slips away.

And I'm walking with him. He's still haunting the city after all these years, since he left the place and never returned. From the age of seventeen, I've been following Lowry down back alleys and into derelict cinemas. When I was working recently with retired merchant seamen on a project called 'The Lighthouse Invites the Storm', about Lowry's decision to leave Liverpool, we watched the tides rise and fall, watched for ships that hardly ever docked here, looked at the rocks and mudbanks of New Brighton where Lowry used to walk, sat in the pubs he drank in.

And he's there, disappearing up the shadowy staircase of the Forum on Lime Street. I recently went inside the Forum, which closed down in 1998. My mother was the secretary for its architect, Alfred Shennan, builder of cinemas and synagogues. And there in the Forum's faded Art Deco splendour I saw ghosts. Perhaps. My mother fleetingly glimpsed by the ice-cream kiosk. Lowry sadly eyeing up the half-demolished Futurist and Scala cinemas on the other side of Lime Street.

If Liverpool is a novel then this chapter is the saddest part. In August 2016, I stood watching the demolition of the Futurist, where my mother took me to matinees when I was young, the cinema that became my own favourite building and which I would use as the setting for my play Bright Phoenix in my own futile attempt to save its life. After a long and deliberate decline, imposed on it by the philistines who run the city, the cinema was disappeared, almost overnight. Standing next to me was Malcolm Lowry's bewildered ghost, confused, battling the Furies, watching Liverpool slowly being erased.

Another ghost – my mother's – walked through the demolition site, sounding a warning against future ruins. Her city was being assaulted once again by fools, and she'd come back to draw attention to their stupidity. *Bright Phoenix* was a hex against these destroyers and a hymn to dreams and dreamers. In the 1960s, the Watchers witnessed the market hall being demolished. And now here I was, some sixty years later, just like them, on the verge of tears, watching *my* palace of dreams being reduced to rubble and dust.

In *Hear Us O Lord from Heaven Thy Dwelling Place* Lowry brilliantly compares Pompeii to the ruins of Liverpool on a Sunday afternoon. And there they are, towering over Lime Street, over half the city – the ruins, the buddleia and rubble and dust. Out of the ashes banal monsters rise in kit-form. Everywhere you look there are cranes. The first thing they build is the lift shaft, rough concrete-slabbed blunt instruments, sky-stabbers like Anselm Kiefer's *The Seven Heavenly Palaces*. But there's nothing heavenly about these ugly shafts in this archaeological era of vapidity; soon they will be clad in even more banal facades, for these are the lift shafts of budget hotels and student accommodation. All of it meaningless, thoughtless and temporary.

If you walk the streets of Liverpool today you can still just about go trespassing by making yourself invisible. If you get lucky, you can climb through a vent and feel your way through the gloom of a cinema or ruined pub. You can walk your way into the stories. You can move like a poltergeist through the dusty corridors of old shipping offices and you can just about still imagine the city that my mother knew, that Lowry knew, the strange arcades of dreamers. This is how I think my way into the city, into 'the Liverpool of the self'.

At the end of a day's wandering my mum and I would queue up in Skelhorne Street bus station, a cavernous place stinking of diesel and doughnuts. These days Skelhorne Street is a nowhere place, an emptiness; thanks to the monstrous slab backside of the new chain hotel on Lime Street it will never see sunlight again. In those days, it was strange and ancient, Hogarthian and dodgy. I can still see the limping pigeons, their feet burnt off from walking through puddles of scalding oil, and the bus conductors having a pint in the station bar, demolished long ago.

And we've all been to the pictures, or the Christmas show, or for Battenberg cake in Lewis's, but I've also been on fire escapes and rooftops and I've seen the city from the edge of the great grey sky.

My mother taught me Liverpool; she was the guide into its shadows, into the hidden and forgotten. When I walk through Liverpool, and when I write and think about it, I summon up my mother and try and see it through her eyes. I have used my blind grandfather in the same way, have tried to *see* the city through his blindness, to feel what he must have felt when the city he knew was being demolished. He would walk through a memory of the city that was no longer there. My mother, grandad and Lowry are connected by imaginative filaments, and together they create a spell. I can't quite explain it – I don't want to explain it. The important thing is that they are alive inside my kaleidoscope of muses and they help me to write and to dream.

My mother is still there, years after her death, up on that fire escape, or walking just ahead of me down Leather Lane and Hackins Hey and leading me into the cinema ruins – the Mother-Muse, flitting through the pages of the city, through its gutted arcades.

Glass Constellations

I remember my grandad's house as being derelict, even though he still lived there. I have a very unstable memory of a Christmas tree, festooned with tinsel, in a front parlour with no ceiling. The plaster and wallpaper are peeling, the lino is worn away, the coal cellar beneath is flooded and raindrops fall into enamel buckets. Uncles sit smoking in the ruins of this terraced house in Everton, in the ruins of a faulty memory, where Kathy Kirby sings 'My Thanks to You' on *Two-Way Family Favourites*.

I remember grandad's and nana's kitchen table, and the mad cabaret surrounding it, at the centre of which stood grandad – I don't remember him ever sitting down – a blind, frail old man who had spent his life with horses. I would sit at the heart of this kitchen, memorising swear words, listening to their secret language, a slang mangled from butcher talk, wartime spiv, car auctioneer and bookies runner code. These were rough-edged Liverpool men, butchers by trade, who lived by their own rules. They wore demob suits and hair grease and they smelled of cheap aftershave, sawdust and meat. In this 1960s memory-world of bleached and muted colours, it feels like the war has never ended and Liverpool is a bomb site. Grandad's house is falling down, the fireplace is alight with burning furniture, and my dad's old accordion is hanging from a nail on the kitchen door ... It's beautiful and strange, it's utterly present, so real that

I could take you there. And when we get there we will be living in a Terence Davies film.

When I first saw Davies's *Distant Voices, Still Lives* I recognised my Liverpool immediately. I half expected to see my grandad, nana and my uncles spilling out onto the doorstep, drunk from a funeral, or singing songs at weddings, dance halls and christenings, comforted by ritual and clan spirit. Just like the people in the film, my family expressed their feelings at weddings and wakes by singing snatches of old show tunes and hymns. Their happiness, sadness and anger were enmeshed in the lyrics of pop songs. Is it that they didn't know what to say? Or is it that a burst of 'Buttons and Bows' or Alma Cogan's 'Dreamboat' says everything that needed to be said?

I've walked through the doors into that film, I've sat in that parlour. I've put up the Christmas decorations as a choir sings 'In the Bleak Midwinter'. I've listened to old women singing, 'If You Knew Susie' in the pub saloon. The women marry the men because they are good dancers. The women laugh and sing their songs and the men move like Clark Gable. They sit round the table like men at a seance, but instead of receiving messages from the dead, they *are* the dead, sending signals to the present, transmissions from the Sundays of 1960s Liverpool, faulty projections onto tattered screens, faulty broadcasts on battered transistor radios.

On Saturdays and Sundays, the uncles would sit at the kitchen table doing the football coupon and 'Spot the Ball' and sharing out the abattoir meat. They'd have the Billy Cotton Band Show, or the wrestling or a western on the telly. The uncles would drink pale ale and the aunties would have a shandy, and there'd always be laughter.

Blind grandad was the poet monologist of pools coupons, head full of horses from when he was a carter down the docks. His closest companion was an enormous Bakelite radio, which he'd sit close to, blind eyes searching the room as if trying to glimpse radio waves … as if he were a milk-eyed receiver of signals sending him horse-racing results and the latest score at Goodison Park.

Uncles spoke of falling bombs and shrapnel, sitting at a table full of ham shanks and brisket, offal and mincemeat, acting out the ritual of guessing where the ball was, and laughing that all we would win was a shilling for the meter.

Brown ale, pale ale, warm rum, boiled milk, boiled-ham sandwiches, cigarettes, Battenberg, meat unwrapped from newspaper and spread out on the table: rib-eye, lamb chops, kidneys, pork belly, pigs' head, liver and heart. We sit laughing at Leon Arras as he grunts and gurns; we boo as Jackie Pallo gets Mick McManus in a headlock, while dad changes the dressings on nana's sore legs. Grandad listens to mum reading him the news, his stick twitching in his battered fingers. The radio in the back kitchen is playing Billy Fury singing 'Wondrous Place', the glory of our Sundays in his song. Mum is dancing, shoes off, shuffling on the lino – pretty, painted mum.

At the centre of it all, nana sat on her bentwood chair, laughing at her family, dispensing cups of tea from the perpetually warmed pot, buttering crusts and rummaging for biscuits in her floral pinafore apron, callinga for the death of Mick McManus. If Cilla Black was on she'd sing along to 'Step Inside Love'. She was a huge woman, smelling of Parma Violets, deaf as a post. The television blasted at full volume on the wild chance she might catch the odd word. Now and then she'd burst into a chorus of 'Sons of the sea, bobbin' up and down like this', complete with hands dancing like boats on stormy water. Lemonade with a spoonful of sugar 'to take away the fizz' was her treat for the kids, and if any of us showed the slightest sign of a cold we'd get a glass of warm rum. I've no idea what sort of a life she'd had, if she'd ever had a job, if she'd ever seen anything of the world. I would sit in an armchair watching, aware of the fragility – and obscenity – of the human body, her legs weeping strange-coloured fluids, my father tenderly attending to her wounds with ointment and gauze. If she saw someone wince at the sight of her lesions as my dad changed the dressings she would mix a tumbler of warm water and a tot of Lamb's Navy Rum and make them drink it, as if the pain belonged to them.

I think, in memories, these people are often dying. The corridors of hospitals are always looming in my thoughts. When I think of my grandparents and uncles they are hardly ever outside in open spaces, they are always in kitchens, butchers' shops, front parlours, hospitals. But in the hospital memories the dying are somewhere down the corridor, because we were never allowed to see them. We knew they were there – by *we,* I mean my sisters and I – because of the whispers. Dying and death were hushed tableaux of handshakes, hands on shoulders, heads in hands, hands drying eyes with handkerchiefs, hands giving children half a crown, hands waving goodbye.

This is what I'm trying to summon up, this psychic weather in some ruined dream-space, this ritual world where the cinema trip and bonfire night have as much mythic and emotional resonance as the hospital visit, the wedding that will inevitably end in tears, the funeral that ends up in the boozer. I watch this mythic Liverpool through a faulty cathode-ray tube, a junk shop of fragmented images, suffused with the glow of burning cigarettes.

And later when the family have gone home my grandfather sits at the kitchen table late at night, the football results and Shipping Forecast seeping into his thoughts as he holds his magnifying glass in his ruined hands; the futile, torn-up pools coupons burning in the ashtray next to the glass of warm rum. He died over forty years ago but he's still sitting there, staring into his blindness in a house full of rain.

This is one of the guiding principles I learnt from Terence Davies – that telling stories that draw on the magic of this, the mosaic of remembering, is a kind of folklore or even mythology. My grandad's house is no longer there, but they can't demolish the meaning and strangeness of the place or the emotional potency of the songs that were sung there. When I sit down to write a story, whatever the time or place of its setting, I subconsciously place myself inside the echo chamber of that ruined house. I think it's the beginning of nearly everything I've written; it has the same potency as the doorway and staircase in *Distant Voices*. In my imagination, I walk into grandad's kitchen, say hello to the old man, throw a piece of broken furniture on the fire and spark up a dog-end from the ashtray: then I can begin.

Grandad had chests of drawers full of light bulbs and radio and television valves. He was an inventor, cannibalising radiograms and Grundig TV sets, blind eyes full of lights that only he could see. In my radio play *Red Rock, Grey Rock* he talks about these glass constellations:

> The stars lend light to the vault of heaven. On this night, the stars have come to us. Old stars I had to unscrew from the heavens, fallen stars I found in the backyard. It was shame to throw what once had been so beautiful away.

He had created his own universe according to the needs of his imagination. The glass valves were a secret luminous treasure, and you could tap them with a spoon and play them like a xylophone, literally the music of the spheres ...

In *Red Rock, Grey Rock* we sit in the attic, imagining that the aurora borealis is leaking in through the skylight like celestial music:

> And it was ... I couldn't see a thing apart from gloom in the grey winter dusk but I was prepared to enter into grandad's world ... out of the scant gleanings of his unhappy mind grandad had created his own universe according to the needs of his imagination ... The city that stretched out all around us was grandad's magic encyclopaedia, and the sky above it was full of clinking icicles of musical light.

These memories are dream-myths, half-forgotten, half-invented legends. And when I grew up I wrote them into – dreamed them into – stories, or perhaps they were dreamed into me, into notebooks, onto envelopes, into radio plays and theatre shows, as archetypes of the kind of liminal characters I love. At first, I didn't want them – I didn't invite these people into the narrative, they just strolled in through the backyard door of stories and dreams, pulled up a chair at the kitchen table and made a wonderful nuisance of themselves.

In the broken magic lantern of memory these ghosts flicker and glow: fragments of psychedelic linoleum, fairground ornaments, men's battered hands, industrial injuries, cigarette butts, wedding rings, dartboards, Brylcreem, swear words, broken hearing aids, fob watches, a blind man's stick and false teeth.

When it rains inside the house in another Davies film, *The Long Day Closes*, I am back inside grandad's house on the last day that I ever visited. The roof is falling through, and the bulldozers and wrecking balls are knocking the terraces down. I am queuing for the cinema in the rain. I've somehow converted these scenes from my past into moving pictures. Fragments of Super 8 film seem to flicker, the colours are desaturated, the nitrate film is unstable, and the celluloid catches fire. The ordinary is destabilised, disrupted, and it's all this ruin and distortion that to me – paradoxically – makes the writing work.

All this noise, ruckus and blare arrives as if transmitted from one of grandad's glowing valve machines. When I remember my family watching a cowboy film there is always someone banging their fist on the television to stop the picture rolling, or hanging the coat-hanger aerial on the ceiling light bulb. And here in the present day I'm doing the same thing: trying to get the picture right – or trying to get it wrong – making an aerial out of twisted wire in order to watch the stories.

The dog on the frozen boating lake, the nest of mice in the side of beef, the accordion wheezing like a lung-beast, the insurance man on his bicycle, the rag-and-bone man's balloons, my dad on the back of a coal truck, worse for wear after one too many tipples, tangled up in his bicycle, the escaped canary flying down Winslow Street, its owner running after it, trying to catch it in a shoebox. The memories are a cosmology of battered images and archetypes, a universe you'd find in a cardboard box at a car-boot sale.

There's a heart-in-mouth sequence in *Distant Voices* – a queue of black umbrellas in torrential rain outside the Futurist Cinema on Lime Street – and then there are two weeping women in the cigarette-smoke-filled dark, followed by two men falling in slow motion through the air, shattering through a skylight to the tune of *Love Is A Many-Splendored Thing.* When I watch this I'm watching my dad falling down a factory chimney on the night I thought he'd die. In three minutes of cinematic magic it summons forth my own ghosts, and in that short space of screen time it does what I've spent thirty years trying to do in my work. It's a poem made from cigarette smoke and magic, and black umbrellas and rain.

I try to make a radio antenna of myself, in order to capture images and turn them into stories, rough around the edges, drunk and unruly, romantic and dancing. They aren't dead, my muses – they never will be. They're in grandad's kitchen, gathered round the table, swigging beer and sharing out the meat.

Fever Hospital

In Liverpool, on a winter's afternoon, I meet a man who is 230 years old. He walks out of bad weather on the hills and stops to ask me if I am a priest. Cadging a cigarette off my friend Horatio, he begins to tell us the city will be the death of us, that the priests and politicians will be the first to go and they'll take the rest of us with them. In all his years, he's never seen the likes of it, and already people are dying on the cold November ground. 'I just found a dead man – just a way up the hill there,' he tells us, and as I'm walking up the track into the undergrowth expecting to find a rotting corpse, I find myself slipping back into my childhood, into memories of walking through the streets that used to be here. And there, in the shadow of the cast-iron church, I meet myself, an eight-year-old boy.

The day before my eighth birthday I went into hospital to have my tonsils removed. The hospital was called John Bagot and I remember it as being a Victorian Gormenghast, up on the hill of Everton Brow, overlooking the city and the river. Some people called it the fever hospital and the name suited it. A miasma of gloom and sickliness emanated from its shadows like ectoplasm. The Brow was a hill of slum terraces, blind courts and tower blocks daubed in Protestant graffiti – *Protestant Boys, King Billy, No Popery!* – taunting the Catholics down the hill in the streets crowding the docks and in the tenements huddled beneath the belching smoke of the satanic Tate & Lyle sugar refinery. I didn't know what any of this meant, but I remember being thrilled by it, as if sensing danger in the shadows. We used to pass below this concrete citadel and the buildings looked formidable; tenements and high-rises loomed over us, vast perimeter walls, blocks of flats named for some reason after great Italian statesmen – Cavour, Mazzini and Garibaldi. And who were the Protestant Boys? And were they watching us as we went down Netherfield Road on the bus?

This is where I'm walking now with my friend Horatio Clare in the hail and driving rain of November 2018, half a bottle of cheap rum in my overcoat pocket, soaked to the skin, up on the Brow in the wastes of the park on the grounds where the slums once stood. Trying to remember the names of pubs – the Atlantic, the Clock, the Tug Boat, Old Stingo, where they sang in *Distant Voices, Still Lives* – mental lists of places, of car journeys in childhood rain. What am I looking for? I'm looking for myself when I was eight.

My parents took me to hospital. I carried a small tartan holdall. Inside it were my pyjamas and a washbag, probably some comics – *The Beezer* or *Topper* and a book, maybe *Redshank's Warning* by Malcolm Saville. My parents said goodbye to me and I changed into my pyjamas. A nurse gave me a drink of milk and I sat on my bed looking at the other children and not knowing how to talk to them. I probably cried, or tried not to cry. The lights went out and I escaped into fretful sleep.

In the morning, I wasn't allowed to eat or drink. I was lonely and homesick and it was my birthday. And then, after hours that seemed like days, two men came and told me to climb onto a bed on wheels. They wheeled me down dark corridors, chatting to each other about football and pools coupons, their voices echoing off the green tiled walls. And then I was left in a room behind a green curtain until the anaesthetist came to see me and prepared to give me an injection. She asked me how old I was and I told her I was eight – eight today. She told me to count backwards from ten, and as I started counting she said, 'Oh, you should have told us it was your birthday! We'd have operated tomorrow.' but I was counting, seven, six, five, four ... and then I fell asleep.

I remember waking up with a feeling that my throat was made of metal. I expected my parents to be there. A nurse put a water jug and a metal bowl on my bedside table. I felt as if I were drowning, not in water but in echoing sound: glass and metal, voices and clanging radiators. I slept restlessly, dreamed I was a small planet in orbit. When my parents finally came they sat at the side of my bed and spoke in whispers about grandad sending his love and so-and-so from school saying hello. They gave me some birthday cards and a book token for Philip, Son and Nephew, and we laughed about how strange it was to be in hospital on your birthday. I didn't really laugh, I pretended.

They didn't stay long – they weren't allowed to stay.

Three days of this, three days the same. The only relief came in the form of bowls of jelly and ice cream 'to soothe the throat'. And then on the last evening at visiting time my parents sat beside the bed and the matron came to talk to us. I remember her as wearing black and having a face like a man. She tidied up the bed and said, 'Jeffrey is going home tomorrow. He'll be traveling in the ambulance with other children.' My mum said, 'How exciting!' I wasn't sure it was exciting, I just wanted to go home.

And then my parents left because they weren't allowed to stay.

The following morning, I changed out of my pyjamas and packed my holdall. After some breakfast the matron came and said, 'All the children who are going home in the ambulance gather your belongings and follow me.' About twenty children followed her, down a flight of stairs and into the ambulance. I sat near the back with my holdall on my lap. I was excited to be going home and I spoke with another boy about how great it was to be in this mad bus.

'Right,' said the matron, 'I'm going to count you all and then you'll be on your way.' She counted us and looked at her clipboard and shook her head and clicked her pen. And then she said, 'There are twenty-one children here and there should only be twenty. Put your hand up if you think you might be the extra child who shouldn't be here.' I sat there, confident I was supposed to be there, because she'd told me and my parents the night before. I felt sorry for whoever wasn't supposed to be there. And then she said she was going to read a list of names, and if our name wasn't on the list we had to put our hand up.

My name wasn't on the list.

She was cross with me. 'Why are you here?' I told her I was there because she told me that I was going home in the ambulance. 'I said no such thing!' She slapped her clipboard as if she were slapping me. She told me to take my bag and go back to the ward. 'Your parents will come and collect you and take you home in the car.' I said we didn't have a car, but she wasn't listening. She apologised to the driver for the delay and pointed up the stairs. A boy laughed as I left the ambulance and I remember walking slowly, heavily up the steps. I walked along corridors, climbed flights of stairs. I was invisible.

I went back to the ward. I sat on a chair at the end of my bed. I remember forcing myself to cry, as if that would make it somehow more bearable. I cried until I was empty.

And then a boy aged about thirteen came into the ward and asked me what I was doing there, and I said I'd been left behind. 'Do you like Marvel comics?' he asked, and I said, 'Yes.'

'Then come with me.'

I followed him to another ward. On his bed was a pile of American comics. *Silver Surfer*, *Batman*, *The Submariner*, *Doc Strange*. I had a look through them; there must have been a hundred of them or more. I picked out a Jack Kirby *Fantastic Four* and sat on the floor just looking at the cover drawing of the Human Torch arcing through the night. And then the tears came again. The boy asked why I was crying, and I said I didn't know where my parents were, and I was afraid I'd never see them again.

He led me to a window and stood me on a wooden chair. Through the window I could see the city and, far away, the sea. 'See down there?' He pointed down the hill towards Everton Valley. 'See that old man, selling the *Liverpool Echo*?' I could see the bent old man. 'Well, when he's sold the last *Echo* in his pile, that man is going to come and get you. Because that man is your new dad.'

For an hour or more I stood on the chair, watching the old man fold newspapers, pass them to customers, pocket the money, exchange a few words. I watched him in his raincoat and trilby, watched him lighting and smoking cigarettes. The pile of newspapers grew smaller until eventually he folded the last one. And then he rolled up his satchel, tucked it under his arm and started walking up the hill towards the hospital. He was coming to get me and take me home to my new life.

I turned to the boy on the bed. He just shrugged as if to say, 'Get over it, kid.' But he had made this happen and I hated him. I would never see my parents again.

The world became two things at once. It became an enormous, endless void like an airless winter desert, stretching on to infinity, a place where everything was new and terrifying and somehow apocalyptic – even though I didn't know what apocalyptic meant. There was an emptiness about that world that was also inside me. Everything was erased, including everything I'd been so far in the eight years I'd existed. My family and friends, the world I knew, the corner shop, the walk to school, the caravan holidays in Prestatyn, the painting of the boat on my bedroom wall, the tea caddies full of toy soldiers, the Brothers Grimm at bedtime, the boating lake, the smell of my mum's compact mirror, the fireplace full of ash, the toast cut into the shape of a house, the smell of grandad's tobacco pouch … all of it erased. And the second thing the world became was the future – darkness and a kind of prison in a cellar, in an old newspaper seller's house of shadows; I could see the dirty fingernails on his gnarled hands.

Then the doors swung open. I closed my eyes; when I opened them again I saw my father. He scooped me into his arms, picked up my tartan holdall and strode towards the stairs. The matron, who looked like a man, came running towards us, shouting, 'You can't just walk in here like this! There are procedures! Put that child down!' He stopped, turned towards her, almost spat, looked at her with eyes on fire. *This is my son and I am taking him home.* And then we were in fresh air and we were going home.

I'm walking now, close to where the hospital once stood. I remember quietly celebrating when I found out it had been demolished. I only noticed it had gone sometime in the 1980s when I went walking up the hill from Great Homer Street market where we had a stall. I had walked up to Netherfield Road, half expecting to see the hospital and then I remember thinking I'd taken a wrong turning. It was a shock. That dreadful day came flooding back.

The hospital is made of shadows. The green tiled stairways echo. I am walking down long corridors and hardly see a soul. I am an eight-year-old boy lost in echoing darkness. I remember it as an animation, a stark, expressionist, jagged, black-and-white cartoon with a screeching violin soundtrack. At the edges of the frame, smudged charcoal daubs of looming shadows transform into monstrous matrons looming over the small boy with his suitcase. The shadows of the old man and the teenage boy are negative spaces into which the child might fall and never re-emerge.

And then the memory slips into the after-days, and I am at home in my bedroom. There are 'Get Well' cards from children at school. I arrange them on the blanket box. I don't think of them as being from friends because these are the children who bully me. I lie in my sick bed and I read my books.

For comfort and some kind of sanctuary from chaos, I read Robert Louis Stevenson's *A Child's Garden of Verses*. I create 'a land of counterpane' in my bed, make hills and valleys and rolling seas of the blankets, and arrange toy soldiers.

When I was sick and lay a-bed,
I had two pillows at my head,
And all my toys beside me lay,
To keep me happy all the day.
And sometimes for an hour or so
I watched my leaden soldiers go,
With different uniforms and drills,
Among the bed-clothes, through the hills;
And sometimes sent my ships in fleets
All up and down among the sheets;
Or brought my trees and houses out,
And planted cities all about.
I was the giant great and still
That sits upon the pillow-hill,
And sees before him, dale and plain,
The pleasant land of counterpane.

My mum comes in and checks on me, plumps up the pillows, arranges the eiderdown. Airfix soldiers tumble over in the seismic collapse of the Calyx-patterned bedspread. In the days following my return home I dread anyone mentioning the hospital. There is a silence around it – a negative space – and I am inside that silence like a boy made of winter.

On a bleak November afternoon, the parkland is barren; only the wind and rain can transform it into a wild place. Out across the bay the sky is aluminium and charcoal, split by rods of silver light. We shelter in the doorway of the cast-iron church. I think I sometimes came here with my mother.

The weather is memory and memory is weather. It seeps into this place, becomes layered into it. The meteorology of memory.

Here I am, walking on July 12 in the 1960s. The drums of the Orange Lodge marching bands provide the musical accompaniment. There are taunting voices, a scuffle, swearing, crowd surging, roaring. I find it all threatening – and exciting.

More than 120,000 people used to live in these streets, but in the 1960s they were forced to move out to new towns, to Skelmersdale, Kirkby and Speke. Then in the 1980s, I remember watching the Brow being cleared and landscaped. In its early days, the park made no sense. The tower blocks stood like desolate ships in a sea of barren topsoil and weeds. *Over your cities grass will grow.* The hill swallowed up places and lives. Everything felt – still feels – provisional.

In 1664, during the English Civil War, Prince Rupert of the Rhine camped here with 10,000 Royalist troops. Wandering the winter-bleak hillside, I can just about imagine it swarming with soldiers, waiting for the order to descend on the city below. Liverpool's population was a little over 1,000, and the city was, in Rupert's words, 'but a Crow's Nest that a parcel of boys could take.' In the bloody attack, Rupert lost 1,500 men, and 360 of Cromwell's troops were killed. After plundering the town, the Royalists hauled the loot back up onto this hillside and buried it in the Everton earth, never to be found.

Horatio and I are fuelled up on rum and Guinness; the wind is hard and full of ice. We have come here today in search of Thomas De Quincey, who lived here in the early 1800s in a house on Everton Terrace, which stood nearby. We look for clues. The metal information boards that described the history of Everton have been removed, presumably stolen and sold to the scrap man. We look out to the Irish Sea, to the wind turbines spinning in a patch of silver sky, the last light of forever. We walk amongst an invisible community of the displaced, of the dead. We are the only people here – apart from that vision striding towards us, draped in a cloak like a revenant monk, banging the path with a wooden staff, and shouldering a rucksack. His eyes are wild, and he's frightened of a dead man in the undergrowth. I go and look, slowly stepping through dead grass and half-buried house bricks towards a body in a snorkel parka slumped on a rat-gnawed mattress. Nervously, I pull back the fake caribou fur hood. I'm relieved to find it's just a heap of fly-tipped rags. But there are shrines here, plastic flowers and trinkets in pound-store vases; prayer cards, scribbled messages to the departed. Are these

memorials to rough sleepers who perished here? Or to people who once lived on these spots where the terraced houses stood?

I go back to Horatio and the revenant, who tells us, 'Go to the mountains, lads! The city will kill you. Go to the distant hills before the city kills us all.' We ask him where he's walking to and he points in the direction of the Welsh mountains and says, 'Ben Nevis'. Then he strides off down the hill with a final wave. Horatio looks at me, joyously, loving the madness of all this. 'Isn't Ben Nevis in Scotland?' I wonder out loud who the hell we have just met, and Horatio shrugs and says, 'Thomas De Quincey'.

The pathway follows the line of the old street and we decide our revenant appeared in exactly the spot where De Quincey left the house each day for his walks to the 'resounding shore' of the Mersey. Allen Ginsberg came here in 1965 with Adrian Henri, hoping to make a mystical connection with William Blake on Albion Street, which runs just below the gates of St George's church. Today, the church is clad in a layer of corrugated tin that bangs in the wind and rattles when it hails. We follow De Quincey down the hill, past the lock-up tower, imagining when this was a village beyond the city and the road we're on was a country lane.

De Quincey is heading for the river and we follow him into his private pandemonium; the opium-eating years. When I first read *Confessions of an English Opium-Eater* in the 1970s I had no idea he had even been in Liverpool. What attracted me to the book was the word *opium,* for in those days I was obsessed with drugs, even though I'd never taken any. I didn't know anyone who *did* take drugs in those days, apart from the boys who went to Northern Soul all-nighters in Wigan Casino and took amphetamines so they could stay awake and dance until daylight. I ingested my drugs through the pages of second-hand paperbacks. I was addicted to William Burroughs's *Junky* and *Naked Lunch;* I got hooked on opium by devouring the pages of Jean Cocteau's diaries. Quite often, I found these books in Great

Homer Street market. No one wanted them. In amongst the
Jean Plaidys and Mills and Boons I'd dig up a copy of Kenneth
Patchen's *Journal of Albion Moonlight* or Annie Dillard's *Pilgrim
at Tinker Creek;* books that became talismans, bibles.

On Great Homer Street in 1847 there were rows of fever
sheds where Catholic priests tended dying typhoid victims. In
February of that year there were 8,000 recorded cases, potato-
famine migrants stricken with a disease caught in the cellars
where they slept. The priests who tended the dying were, in turn,
killed by the fever.

In his walks to the river, De Quincey passes this way. Some
days he walks beyond Bootle on the shore, or 'rambles about on
the pier'. He reads Cowper's *Iliad,* the Bible, Wordsworth and
Coleridge. Sometimes he reads aloud 'to the ladies' from *The
Winter's Tale.* He visits a man named Williams on Duke Street
where he drinks 'a few teaspoons full of ginger wine'. He goes to
church. He appears to be bored and restless and his diaries are
little more than lists of things done, people met, books read. He
reads *The Odyssey* and finds that 'independent of the insipidity
of the story, there is no character in it.' He writes lists of books
he wants to write, which include an essay on Julius Caesar and a
'poetic and pathetic ballad reciting the wanderings of two young
children and their falling asleep on a frosty moonlit night among
the lanes ... and so perishing.' He wants to write about a man
'dying on a rock in the sea ... which he had swum to from a
shipwreck ... within sight of his native cottage and his paternal
hills'. There are glimpses of stories in his diaries. On his way
to church he sees 'people running after a mad dog; – am again
disturbed by old man'. He walks through Kirkdale and Walton,
where he shelters from the rain under a hedge. He writes to
Wordsworth expressing his admiration for the *Lyrical Ballads.*
And every day he walks, 'by French prison and lane, to windmill
on shore'. On Saturday, June 4, 1803, he goes 'to the same fat
whore's as I was at the last time; – give her 1s, and a cambric

pocket handkerchief; – go home miserable.' On June 9 he writes, 'misery is a glorious relief – a delight!' He sounds like any other eighteen-year-old man having an existential crisis and wallowing in divine misery. He sounds like *me* when I was eighteen.

At Cazneau Street, Horatio and I pause and try to work out which route De Quincey would have taken. In 1803 this area would have been nothing but fields rolling down to the river. By the shore, people bathed on holidays, perhaps taking a drink in the hostelry owned by a Dutchman named Vandries, whose 'house of entertainment became well known'. Where did De Quincey find his 'fat whore'? Perhaps in Vandries' house of entertainment. In the ruins of Clarence Dock, we try to imagine the 'wilderness of sandhills' that used to be here. There were fishermen's cottages and men and women taking the plunge in the cold waters of the Mersey. We walk past auto-repair lock-ups and an old pub converted into a convenience store. We have lost the trail of De Quincey and we can't get to the shore for all the fenced-off building sites.

Somewhere nearby, in February 1940, Brendan Behan is woken by the landlady of the bed and breakfast that he's staying in: 'It's not a pleasure trip; he's come to blow up the Liverpool docks'. In *Borstal Boy* he tells it like a farce and you can picture the staging of it as the landlady shouts up the stairs, 'Oh God, oh Jesus, oh Sacred Heart. Boy, there's two gentlemen to see you.' He knows 'by the screeches of her that these gentlemen were not calling to enquire after my health, or to know if I'd had a good trip. I grabbed my suitcase, containing Pot. Chlor, Sulph Ac, gelignite, detonators, electrical and ignition, and the rest of my Sinn Féin conjuror's outfit, and carried it to the window. Then, the gentlemen arrived.' He's only been in Liverpool a day and he's arrested and sentenced to three years. He's a child terrorist, here to blow up ships. In borstal, to his great surprise, he is treated with great civility when they could have treated him like scum. As Fintan O'Toole says, 'the evil Brits deprive him of the glory of martyrdom by treating him remarkably well.'

We head into town, where we drink rum in a pub full of tattooed men wearing Union Jack T-shirts. We make sound recordings of the streets. The last I see of Horatio, he is running down Lime Street, his microphone held before him like a divining rod as he captures the sound of two police horses, their hooves clattering on the tarmac. It's dusk in Liverpool, the streets are cold and the pavements are greasy with dirt and sleet. In *Confessions of an English Opium-Eater* De Quincey writes, 'I put up a petition annually, for as much snow, hail, frost, or storm, of one kind or another, as the skies can possibly afford us.' I head for the pub, walking through his weather.

Chimney Birds

At the exact moment my father was falling down the inside of a factory chimney I was falling headlong over the handlebars of my bicycle and onto the loose gravel of a road. Round about this time we had been to the circus, where I saw Billy Smart standing at the entrance to the big tent, elegant in waistcoat and fob watch, fat cigar between his teeth. Beautiful women came riding into the ring on elephants, wearing diamante leotards and birds-of-paradise feathers in their beehive hairdos. As I lay stunned on the gravel and a man came running out of his house to scoop me up in his arms and carry me to his kitchen, the vision that flooded my semi-conscious mind was of elephants and women with feather plumes in their hair. Gravel had scraped my forehead and the impact of the fall had given me concussion.

When I got home I was aware something had happened because the kitchen door was blocked by a neighbour called Muriel, who wouldn't let me in the house. I sat on the path with my mangled bike and waited and watched. I became distinctly aware of the blue veins on the woman's thighs. Time stretched into infinity until I was eventually allowed into the house where my mother sat on the sofa, surrounded by too many neighbours. She was drying her eyes and then she was tucking her handkerchief into her sleeve and smiling at me. *Your dad has had an accident...*

Owls flying above rooftops, calling the names of the soon-to-be-dead in the dark. And often in the night the chimney birds would come. You could hear them fluttering in the boarded-up fireplace. Then he would withdraw his hand and in the nest of his fingers there would be one, sometimes two, naked birds, scraggy bundles of bird bones, twisting, beaks agape, coated in ash and dust.

Every time we go to see my dad, I tell my daughter to remember to look at his hands. His eyes are ice-blue and when I was young I found them difficult to look into, and so I used to look at his hands: dirty fingernails, factory-worker's palms, sometimes holding a rescued sparrow. His hands, big as hawk's wings, were the hands of a kind man.

My mum told me that my dad had fallen down the inside of a chimney stack in the factory where he worked. It didn't make any sense. His job was on the factory floor, making *Eagle* comics. Why was he climbing up the inside of a chimney? Perhaps he was rescuing birds at work as he always did at home ...

When I go to bed that night and close my eyes, this is what I see: three men falling, one of them my father, each man hitting a scaffolding plank with a dull thud, then another plank, then another, each thud breaking things inside the men, knocking the air out of their lungs, folding up their bodies, plummeting downwards through dust, creosote, birds' nests, pigeon bones, soot. Then, one by one, they land in bird shit and rubble in the furnace and lie there in a broken heap. I see these images on the inside of my eyelids, and when I go to sleep they remain there in the form of nightmares. I convince myself that my father is going to die. And this is when I discover what he means to me. I am grieving for him while he's still alive and this must mean I love him. I have headaches because of my own accident. I don't go to school. My head bleeds. I imagine I have somehow caused my father's fall by going over the handlebars of my bike.

My mother liked to sing. On Sundays she would take her leather-bound hymn book down from the shelf and sing along to

Songs of Praise on the television, even though she said she no longer believed in God, not since my grandfather's horrible death in what we called 'the lung ward'. But she would sing along anyway: 'God of Mercy, God of Grace', clear as a choirgirl, while her children buried their heads in comics, pretending to be embarrassed. When my dad was in hospital my mother didn't sing.

Sometimes I remember those waiting days – the grieving-for-a-death-that's-yet-to-come days – in the old house, even though it all happened in the new house. I wonder if the darkness of the old parlour and lobby were more suited to the memory-mood of grieving? Perhaps the three long days of thinking my dad was going to die weren't suited to the clear light of the new house. I carry both houses inside me and sometimes they change places. The new house has a bathroom but I remember the tin bath hanging on the backyard wall. The tin bath in front of the coal fire, pots and pans of water boiling on the cooker, the family taking it in turns – in age order – to have the weekly bath. My dad stretched out in the tin bath in the kitchen; steam clouds from cooking pots, coal fire burning, 'Laughing Policeman' on the gramophone, mum pouring water from the kettle, scalding dad's toes. But the new house doesn't have a coal fire and hot water comes from taps and the tin bath is now the dog's bath for when he runs wild in ditches. Memory is shifting, dissolving.

I stand outside the house where my sisters, Val and Kathryn, and I were born and everything feels unstable, shimmering. Inside the house is a memory of a bedtime when the downstairs rooms were a maze of laundry drying on clothes maidens, the fire flickering and smoking. I can remember a particular night, my mother doing the ironing while I played Robin Hood in the Nottingham Forest of damp underwear. I remember the way my mum would press the back of her hand against her forehead, an almost religious image of fatigue and beauty. I remember the faded roses on her apron. What I can't remember is her body – by which I mean I don't recall her being pregnant. But in the morning when I woke to go to school I could hear a baby crying and my younger sister Kathryn had been born. They must have told me I was going to have a sister but I have no memory of the telling.

I stand outside the house, the place where I enjoyed being ill. My favourite illness was jaundice. My parents made a bed up for me in the front room downstairs. For some reason connected with the illness I wasn't allowed to drink milk. I remember eating bowls of dry Frosties, reading *The Beano* and sleeping in a druggy slumber, dreaming of dead jellyfish on Prestatyn beach. Memory monsters loom, cathode demons who lived in faulty televisions. Leslie Crowther brandishing *Crackerjack* pencils, gurning Hughie Green, sweating Eamonn Andrews, Jackie Pallo spitting blood, yodelling Frank Ifield. And out of this fog and fever come poets. Coleridge's *Ancient Mariner* takes his place alongside Captain Scarlet and the Mysterons in my private, fevered mythology. Gerard Manley Hopkins comes to me out of a school textbook looking like Doctor Strange in his Cloak of Levitation. Hallucinations coloured by swollen glands, tonsillitis and dentist gas. Over and over again, I see the dog on the frozen boating lake and dream of Yuri Gagarin circling the earth. Elsie Barmaid, my very own Molly Bloom, murmurs *yes and yes and yes and yes and yes.*

And birds: I remember holding them, looking at their strange skin and the fragile bones beneath. I found it frightening – the responsibility of protecting such delicate life. More often than not, the birds I held were dead, and no matter how hard I wished them back to life that's how they stayed. We would bury them in the yard and mark their graves with ice-lolly sticks; a small cemetery of birds. When my dad was in the hospital I had nightmares about chimneys, falling, the deaths of birds.

And then, in the new house on the outskirts of the city, on the day of my father's accident, the neighbours drink tea and mither and whisper. I imagine myself falling down and down, through grief and dust. Eventually the news comes and my mother's eyes are bright with a different kind of tears. The thing is, he *doesn't die*. He hasn't had a heart attack, he has been asphyxiated by gas fumes, and in his falling he has unbalanced the two other men and they have dropped down the throat of the chimney like aerialists falling from the flying trapeze in Billy Smart's circus. And I decide that my nightmares have magically saved him. By imagining the fall, I have metamorphosed his death into a kind of falling sleep that saves his life. And once again my mother sings on Sundays.

Years after my dad's accident I realised I hadn't fallen headlong over the handlebars of my bicycle at the same time that my father was falling down the inside of a factory chimney. In reality, these two accidents happened several years apart but I had conflated them in my mind, perhaps as a way to bring two dramatic events together, improving on the facts to heighten the memory. I can see myself flying over the handlebars, hitting the gravel. I can see my dad falling at exactly the same moment. He is falling like a broken bird.

The Transit Camp Ophelia

The girl had a Second World War silk parachute and she would wear it like a wedding dress. She made the world change colour, pale sheets of fabric erasing the known world as she danced like a young Isadora Duncan.

We'd gone to live on a new housing estate – or rather, a still-being-built housing estate – that butted up against a hillbilly farmyard. There were two burnt-out holiday coaches dumped in the middle of overgrown potato fields, and there was a sandy-bedded brook full of frogs and newts. There were outhouses where I imagined great train robbers holed up while they shared out the loot. The farm fields were disappearing, buried beneath semi-detached houses and roads named Hill Crest, Dell Field and Briar. At the edge of the estate there were the ruins of a Second World War transit camp. People said Polish people lived there, the families of men from places called Warsaw and Gdańsk, men who had fought on 'our side' during the war. Years later I found out that they had been liberated from forced labour and concentration camps, were sent to England in 1946 and came to live in the north of Liverpool in camps built for people made homeless by the Blitz. There are photographs of children at a fete in the late 1940s wearing traditional Polish costumes. Some of these children must have been the parents of the Polish kids I went to school with: farm labourers, Dunlop factory hands. Sometimes at the shops you'd hear women talking in a strange and beautiful language – women who'd been in Nazi labour camps, forced to work in the fields of Germany and Austria; people who had fled from the Russians they feared as much as the Germans. It never occurred to me that these people were here because of fear. They lived in houses just like us and the transit camp that had sheltered them was now a ruined playground.

We used to sneak in through the ripped perimeter fence and explore the overgrown buildings. It was a frightening, mysterious place, a place where we were not supposed to go. Standing stones of ruptured concrete, rusted fence posts, steel hawsers, ruined air-raid shelters; a strange derelict garden designed by Derek Jarman. You could climb down into the cellars and sewers and crawl into claustrophobic chambers full of insects. You could stage running battles with kids from rival estates using rocks as bombs and oil-drum lids as shields, battling for control of the mud hill like feral boys in an overspill *Lord of the Flies*.

Our new house had a garden, a bathroom and an indoor toilet, and the half-built houses beyond our road were places to build dens and hide away from the cocky watchman. Most of all there was the girl. We'd only lived in the new house for a few days and Val had already made friends with her. She took me to the girl's house one day and we played in a shed that smelled of creosote and Swarfega. Her dad was a knife grinder and his tools were in there, too; strange machines out of fairy tales, sharp blades like murder weapons. This new world was so different to the streets I was used to, but in this world, there was a pretty girl who danced slowly wearing yards and yards of silk. Once, in her bedroom she took it out of the wardrobe, spread it across the bed. She disappeared into it, as if into silk-mist, as if into memory. I don't know where she is in the world. I wonder if she remembers how it made me feel, to see a pretty girl disappearing into a cloud of silk.

One day she calls my name on the road and I follow her. She's carrying the parachute and an old lady's handbag. We walk in silence to the transit camp. In her handbag she carries the pendulum weight from a grandfather clock. Sometimes she doesn't even speak to me, she just drifts through the building site, through the mud, across the wooden plank bridges, over the ditches, through the rip in the perimeter fence, into the field, down into the vandalised drains of the transit camp, down amidst the insects. I watch her, she turns and glances, as if I am a passing thought that has just occurred to her. That glance makes me exist, makes me into something or someone that matters. I follow her.

She brings her father's sharpening steel and stones. She places them on a corrugated sheet and lays a decaying bird between the tools. They look like weapons that have killed the bird. *The anxiety of this moment.* I want to touch her. I want to say her name, the magic spell of *Lizzie, Lizzie.* I want the feeling of anxiety to continue, I want to feel the tension of the moment in my body, I want to *nearly* touch her, to not touch her, I want to turn and run away.

A Roman candle flares in the half-built house. It's late October and the air smells of gunpowder. We live in a state of constant truancy. Our mothers think we have gone to Sunday school. This field of weeds and ruins is our kingdom. We are streaked with dirt and tears, our fingertips are burnt, we smell of urine. We crawl inside an oil drum and press our bodies together, bellies stained with rust.

We find half-full tins of paint and spill the contents into the dirt. She stirs the paint into the earth with a stick, gouging into the mud and spiralling the paint down into the earth, as if drilling it into the very planet. And all the time, she is singing – strange murmurs, *tra-la-la, tra-la-la,* a lullaby nonsense song that seems to add to the pagan ritual.

She takes tadpoles out of the ditch and puts them in her pockets. Her deep kiss is a tadpole kiss, amphibian, larval. I wake up, look at the ink stains on my skin: black tadpole daubs.

She spreads the parachute on a patch of scrub and gravel surrounded by grass growing tall enough to make our den a secret. She opens up the handbag, paints rouge on her cheeks and bright-red lipstick on her mouth. She scatters daisy chains, dandelion clocks, thistledown on the silk, wraps herself in it, laughing.

Then she pulls me towards her, her fingers daubed with lipstick and mascara – and I succumb. We kiss, and when the kissing is over she rolls me off her parachute and begins to pack away her things, waving me away. I watch her from the long grass as she carefully folds up the parachute, smiling to herself, singing softly. She is a housing-estate Ophelia, scattering sweet-wrappers and wilting weeds instead of rue and rosemary, columbine and violets.

Mum's voice is calling, 'It's nearly time for tea, it's nearly time, where are you?' I abandon my Ophelia and run home down the jiggers and ditches.

At the bottom of our road there was an enormous, wide-armed oak tree. To have a tree growing in such close proximity to my new home when I'd been used to the terraced streets of the city was magical and strange – trees belonged in parks, not at the end of the street. A few days after we moved into the new house I went to have a closer look at the tree, climbed over a rickety fence and discovered the brook. I dipped my fingers in the cool water, watched the currents ripple over the silt. All knowledge was there, everything I needed to know. The place was like a watery chapel, a dappled interior echoing with my heartbeat. I felt like I was becoming an animal, the creature I had always wanted to be. And there in the sandy sludge I saw a frog – the first I'd ever seen. I crouched to have a closer look, my eye close to its eye, entering into it. I scooped it up, cupped it in my hands, almost kissing it.

We go spying on a neighbour, me and a boy called Christo, a Catholic boy who spits at God. We are commandos in the mud, crawling through weeds and ditches, down along the fence and saying fuck and spitting. The woman walks slowly. Softly behind her the man walks. We watch her in the derelict transit camp, kissing the man from the off-licence.

A few days later I went back to the kissing den and set the grass on fire with a magnifying glass. I burnt things – a Batman model I had bought in Blackpool, dolls I had found in military pillboxes. I remember watching in horror as the flames caught the weeds and moved in the direction of the building site. My Eden was on fire and I was the firestarter.

I dreamed of Russian tanks on the streets of Prague. I woke with a feeling that the world was nearly over. I remember someone's whispered words, *we will be done for, done to by others*, and I believe that it will happen. We listen to the radio. I don't understand it. I don't want whatever it is we have to end. I walk with the dog to the transit camp and I lie down in the dirt. The perimeter fence casts shadow-patterns on my arms and hands; the dog rummages in the scrub and junk. It could all fade away, I could disappear and nobody would notice. But then I see a turquoise ribbon tied on the dead tree, and I remember Lizzie.

When I am seventeen, I will sit beneath Southport pier with a girl who looks just like Lizzie, and I will kiss her once, lightly on the lips. Above our heads we will hear the sound of Jimmy Radcliffe's *Long After Tonight Is All Over* coming from the Northern Soul night at the Dixieland Showbar. When we walk along the sand to the dunes we won't know what to say to each other, and when we lie down in the dunes I will place my hand lightly on her belly and that will feel like everything a boy could ever need. I will remember forever the blonde hairs on her skin, her hair smelling of sea salt and lavender. And, after walking back into town, and riding on the dodgems, and shyly saying goodbye, I will watch her go home on the top deck of a bus to wherever she lives and I will never see her again.

Today, returning to these places after many years away, I cannot find my bearings. Nothing remains of the transit camp or the abandoned farms. Everything is gone: the tanks and flags of our imagined Czechoslovakia, the watery chapel of the brook, now buried beneath tarmac. But then, as Jimmy Radcliffe's heart-breaking song drifts through my memory I catch a glimpse – a trick of the light – of the transit camp Ophelia, falling through eternity, wrapped in parachute silk.

The Truant Zone

Once in the graveyard beside the canal I found two bodies – the first was a wren in a bower of autumn leaves, the other a shrew, a tiny cat-gnawed ghost. I'd never seen a living shrew or wren and now I held them in my hands, dead creatures, beautiful and strange, hardly weighing a thing, as if their insides had been scooped out with spoons. The shrew was eyeless, light as parchment, the wren was perfect, apart from a snapped-off leg, and I remember feeling sad and enchanted as I carried them down the towpath to the bridge where the bigger boys smoked. I showed them to a boy named Hodge, who always smelled of phlegm, and we laid them out on his dirty handkerchief, side by side so that they looked like a married couple in a pornographic Beatrix Potter, asleep in a nightmare bed. Hodge prodded them, breathed on them, grew bored and went back to smoking dog-ends with the boot boys. If you hung around too close to these boys you'd end up in the cut, so I gathered up my dead creatures and pressed on up the towpath, to the 'truant zone'.

I was always drawn to the canal, to the undersides of its bridges where the wild boys lurked, and beyond that, as it cut through and into the landscape, a portal into a world beyond permission. When I was there I felt unauthorised – a trespasser and a runaway hidden in a cloak of invisibility, out into the fields where no one knew me, where there was no one to know me. It was a kind of exhilarating – or *exhilarated* – madness.

I remember the first time I ever experienced these feelings of being truant. One summer's day I was playing on the school field in the lunch hour and on the far side of the perimeter fence I saw clumps of blackberries in the hedgerow of an abandoned farm, so I crawled through the fence and sat there in the dirt devouring them. It felt like a scene from a prisoner-of-war film. No one knew I was there. I could hear the other children playing, and this was the most frightening, thrilling feeling I think I'd ever had. If nobody could see me then the chances were that I did not exist.

I got back below the fence just in time for the bell, and I went to the classroom and sat at my desk. The teacher looked at me with curiosity and said: 'You've been out of school without permission.' I denied it, I lied to her. She couldn't possibly know. She came up to me and took hold of my stained hands. 'Have you been eating blackberries?' I nodded. 'Any child who's eaten blackberries must have been – without permission – in the old farm field.'

I look into my memory and watch the boy I used to be. He is walking across the rough field on his way to school where he will be bullied for losing David Edwards' fountain pen. He knows where certain birds are and he likes the bit where the path becomes sandy like a beach. Sometimes he meets Ramshaw here, a boy who doesn't want to go to school. They share their sweets and say nothing much at all. But most of the time he is alone. He doesn't want to be lonely but he wants to be alone. Across a broken wall there is a ruined garden with a pear tree. He believes he is the only boy who knows about this tree, and every day he picks a pear and eats it on the way to school. It tastes delicious, like vanilla and lemon. When he gets to school he will be beaten up in the cloakrooms.

Through a backyard gate I see a boy wearing flying goggles and sitting in a dustbin. He is sitting at the controls of a Lancaster bomber, issuing instructions to his ground crew, who scurry about attending to final details. When the boys see they take me prisoner and threaten to execute me as an enemy spy. They argue about who will kill me and one of the boys says he killed the last spy they captured and doesn't want any more blood on his hands. The aeroplane is built out of dustbins, an old mangle and clothes maidens; the joystick is a yard brush. One of the boys – his name is Murray – sees something in me worth saving and before I know it I'm invited on the flight. We have to lick a battery to give the plane power. We pass the battery from hand to hand, from tongue to tongue and then we taxi down the runway. The junkyard bomber is heavy in the air. We do not ride the wind, we break the air apart, *ROGER. TEN FOUR. OVER AND OUT!*

I have made some friends and we are flying to the stars.

Me and a boy called Bernard are on an adventure, lighting Swan Vestas to help us see in the dark. We kneel down in the cold earth inside the canalside military pillbox. The sun shoots in through the gun slits. There is always pornography in pillboxes. Who are the men who come here in the dark? What if they turn up and discover us looking through their magazines? We leaf through them, obsessing over vital statistics, 36–24–36; 38–24–36. We read them out loud, it's exciting. We pay more attention to the numbers than the pictures of the women. We go out into the sunlight and walk down the towpath, and I'm thinking, *if they decide to start the war again we are ready for them,* because the pillboxes and tank traps are still in place. The war is in the living room, Vietnam bleeding from the television and invading the evening meal until mum switches it off and the family return to supper in the suburbs of Liverpool. I think of jungles on fire, terrifyingly beautiful yellows and reds, children running and burning. I am fascinated by this war but I don't know what it is. No one ever talks about it.

The tanks roll into Prague.

On the gates of the canal lock, a stone's throw from the tobacco factory, a storm-battered cormorant hangs its wings out to dry. I walk towards it slowly and crouch down on the gravel path. The bird suddenly drops into the lock water like a drunk in a wet overcoat. I creep towards the edge of the lock and peer down into the dark water. No sign of the bird at first, but then it rises up to the surface, churning the murk, thrashing amongst pop cans and takeaway cartons, almost pulling the water up with its body, a desperate panic. For a few seconds, it hurtles up and down the lock from gate to gate, and then it opens up a space in the water and disappears inside it, thrashing and churning and making an abysmal mess of garbage and dirt. When it comes up to the surface again there is something else entangled in the flotsam – the dead body of a second cormorant, broken-winged and floating face down in the chaos. The diver forces itself out of the lock, up onto the gate and hangs there, looking down into the water where the dead bird floats for a moment or two, until the churning settles and it sinks beneath the surface. And then the whole tormented ballet starts again, and it occurs to me that the diving bird is trying to save the dead bird's life, or pull it out of its death and into the world of living. I watch this terrible ritual for ten, twenty minutes, feeling helpless, bewilderingly awestruck and emotional. I can't take it anymore and walk away, but glance back once to see the crow of the sea preparing to plunge once more into the plastic-bottle flotsam, into the burial water, again and again.

The tanks roll into Prague and Bernard and I get the wars confused. When the news is on television I only half watch it. Every time my mother sees me looking at the Vietnam war she turns the TV off. So it's hard to know why the American boys in helmets are shooting people in rice fields, and setting forests and children on fire in a place that's full of helicopters, phosphorus bombs and water buffalo. And somewhere around this time there are Soviet tanks on the streets of Prague, and Jan Palach sets himself alight in Wenceslas Square. Bernard and I are excited, but we're frightened too. We recite the names of guns – *Ithaca 37, Remington, Winchester* – and we say things like, *fragmentation grenade, rocket launcher* as we crawl through the hedgerows and ditches of the fields on the edge of the city. The war is a waking dream where Soviet tanks are rolling into Liverpool like floats on student rag week.

In the living room Bobby Kennedy is shot with a 22-calibre revolver and then he's lying dead, rosary beads in his hand. My parents are whispering and suddenly Ena Sharples is in the living room instead of death. When I go to sleep Vietnam and Prague and Kennedy are in my dreams. My mother wakes me and my sister Val and opens the curtains. Over the rooftops, around the chimney, there's a shadow-play of owls.

In the hollow of a tree I curated a museum of artefacts, a cabinet of curiosities exhibited inside the body of an oak, its walls charcoal-charred where someone had lit a fire.

Airfix fighter planes have crash-landed in the garden bonfire, down near the graves of hamsters and rabbits. I love the smell of melting fuselage, a weird mix of petrol and cough mixture, and when the plastic Lancaster bomber, Spitfires and Messerschmitts collapse in the flames it's as if strange globular insects have hatched, toxic fireflies floating above the lawn, up and away into the suburban blue. These model airplanes used to hang from my bedroom ceiling on lengths of cotton thread; a Battle of Britain suspended over my pillow. Now, in some unexplainable act of ritual destruction, I have decided to send them crashing into the fire.

In the pillbox, alone in the dark, I scope through the gun-slit watching for snipers. The man who stashes his porn is coming, I can hear boots on the towpath gravel. I grab my bike and ride, terrified of the pillbox man and the war.

Poverty Lane railway bridge was the drop-edge to the far beyond. When we first moved to the new house the land beyond the bridge was a mirage – an unknown, unknowable territory of fields and mist and distant high-rise towers. But soon I was an avid explorer and trespasser – a tree-climber, stalker of rabbits and canal voles, observer of moped thieves. One day, I cycled fast down the hill straight into a swarm of bees. I fell from my bike, screaming, trying to brush them off. I ripped open my shirt and they were crawling over my chest. I danced a wild jig, slapping them dead. Somehow I escaped without a single sting.

This cloud of bees became the portal to the truant zone. I never saw the swarm again, but this is where I would come to disappear. This is where I'd get lost. Sometimes I would lie on the earth and feel the rain or dew seeping through my clothes. Sometimes I'd search ditches and flooded bomb-pits for insects and newts. One day I saw a boy called Hoppy carrying a Tupperware box through a field. Inside the box there was a fat perch. He said he was taking it home to weigh it on the bathroom scales and send a photograph in to *Angling Times*. I knew the fish would die and wanted to rescue it, but instead, because I was unnerved by the stench of cigarettes coming from his mouth, I just watched Hoppy walk away.

I became the ditch-crawler version of myself, moving slowly through weeds, absorbing algae and the smell of stale water into my jeans, into my skin. Pylons hummed. There was the drone of crop-dusters. Alien encounters.

Get up speed on your Raleigh bike and hurtle down the far side and you're on your way to Balls Wood and potato farms. Beyond that is the lunatic asylum – *the mental hospital* – where the sirens wail when men escape into the surrounding fields. The hospital fascinates me. I cycle to its perimeter fences and try and imagine what's going on inside. I imagine violence and schizophrenic hell. Sometimes I see crocodiles of patients from its 'epileptic colony' in the Central Square shopping centre; they wear safety helmets and move slowly past Woolworths and NEMS music shop like sleepwalkers. After the First World War, over 3,000 soldiers were treated here for shell shock and it was considered at the time to be a cutting-edge facility for the study of 'abnormal psychology'. But now it was a place of ill treatment, rumours and dark atmospheres.

Balls Wood is good for dirt-tracking on pushbikes. It's out of bounds because dodgy blokes walk their dogs here, but we go anyway, drawn to its dangers. In the fields around the wood we steal

potatoes and eat them raw. Sometimes we maraud through fields
and ditches on our bikes, and sometimes the sirens go off and we
wait as long as we dare, as long as it takes for the mad men to reach
us and do God knows what. And when we've waited so long that
we're practically wetting ourselves with excitement and fear, we leg
it, pushing our bikes through the ploughed-up earth, pockets full
of spuds, shooting glances over our shoulders.

In the summer mum and dad take us to the hospital's summer
fete. As we walk down the path to the bric-a-brac stalls I can
see a man's hands poking through an open window and hear a
soft voice singing a slow-motion *Hokey Cokey ... Knees bent, arms
stretched ...* The fete is opened by Jimmy Savile, who makes a joke
about the place being full of loonies and tells us to make sure you
all get out at the end of the day. He's wearing a red tracksuit and
enormous gold medallions. He looks as if he's naked beneath his
unzipped top and his hair is bleached, white as washing powder.
There is gymnastic equipment for children to play on and Jimmy
leaps over the vaulting horse, applauded by the laughing crowd. It
is summer, benign and sunlit. All is right with the world.

Shadow Boy

Down the canal, a shadow-boy follows me, scrawny, in a dirty school uniform. His face always looks tear-streaked, as if he had been crying and has wiped city dust across his face with a sleeve. And he looks tired all the time, the sort of boy who falls asleep in Geography and gets slapped with the back of Mr Ashby's hand. Sometimes I see him skulking in the park near our house, by the swings where some lads burnt their school uniforms after they were expelled. When he sees me looking he sticks two fingers up, a *fuck you* to the world. His name is Billy Casper.

I found him on the cover of a book. *A Kestrel for a Knave* changed everything. Every month I would order a book from a school reading magazine. I'd never heard of Barry Hines but I liked the sound of the story and the catalogue had a picture of a kestrel on its cover. *The Observer's Book of British Birds* was one of my favourite books and I recognized the slate-grey and brown hawk, even knew its Latin name, *Falco tinnunculus tinnunculus*. But when the book arrived it had a different cover, a grainy photograph of a boy with a hacked-at haircut and the two-finger salute of the insolent truant. He looked like half the boys I went to school with; he looked like *me*.

'Billy Casper is a boy with nowhere to go and nothing to say.' As I started to read the book I began to see him everywhere. He was a shadow by the lock-up garages. He was a kid helping the milkman, riding on the milk float and spitting in the empties. He was the rough-arsed kid following me down the canal and dipping for tropical fish in the Hotties where the Tate & Lyle factory spewed hot water into the cut. On an enforced cross-country run across the fields I saw him hanging on a tyre swing underneath a half-built motorway bridge. In bed at night I looked around my room and 'the window was a hard-edged block the colour of the sky ... the darkness was of a gritty texture. The wardrobe and bed were blurred shapes in the darkness. Silence.' My bedroom was just like Billy's room at the start of the story, except that my room was full of books. I don't think it had ever occurred to me that people from the north wrote books.

Barry Hines led me to Alan Sillitoe. *Saturday Night and Sunday Morning* might be the first grown-up book I ever read, apart from sneaky reads of my dad's Harold Robbins and Len Deighton books. I read *Billy Liar* and laughed as Billy dumped the calendars he had forgotten to post, reminding me of the rainy day I got fed up lugging my paper sack and dumped fifty *Liverpool Echo*s behind an electricity substation. I borrowed – and never returned – Stan Barstow's *A Kind of Loving* and I recognised my future – my *intended* future – in its pages. I was a boy who would flunk out of school and be sent by the dole to a filing-clerk job at the Council. *The Loneliness of the Long Distance Runner* inspired me to stop running just before the finish line on a district sports day, the act of defiance that finally got me kicked off the cross-country team.

Billy Casper was roaming the fields and I went with him. We were invisible boys. No one in school or at so-called Careers Day cared if we existed. Until I met Billy I don't think I'd ever even seen a hawk, but in some way my passionate obsession with art and books was similar to Billy's identification with a bird. It mattered, and that meant that *I* mattered and so did my desire to create. When Billy flies the hawk he discovers new things about himself, things that were buried inside like dignity, native intelligence, love, hope and spirit. When I saw the film version of the book it almost exactly mirrored the boy and the world I had imagined. My life was being transformed by an act of imaginative engagement.

We went on a school trip to the Odeon in Liverpool to watch *Kes,* the film of the book. *My book!* John Cameron's music was beautiful; bird in flight, soul in flight. Listening to it fifty years later it still moves me to tears. Flutes and clarinets, fragile creatures, airborne. It is the music of Billy's dreams, soaring across the fields on thermals of longing, just beyond his reach. After seeing the film, whenever I read the book I could hear John Cameron's music. In a way, it has become the soundtrack to my own childhood. When I picture myself as a fourteen-year-old boy I hear the fragile call of Harold McNair's flute.

David Bradley *is* Billy Casper. I feel like I'm sitting in the classroom, listening to him talking about the bird. I look at the faces of those boys at their desks, watching them slipping under Billy's magical spell. I look around the cinema and the boys on the school trip are interchangeable with the boys on the screen. I will never know what it's like to fly a bird, but I *do* know what it feels like to discover I have dreams.

Many years later I made a Radio 4 drama documentary called *The Hunt for Billy Casper.* I went on a journey around Britain and spoke to the author, Barry Hines, and the director of the film, Ken Loach. I visited the school that Billy Casper reluctantly attended and it looked exactly like the school where I spent my invisible five years. Barry Hines took me to the farm where Billy climbed the wall to steal the hawk. I could *see* Billy clambering up as I stood there with Barry and my producer Melanie Harris. I felt I was both communing with Billy *and* exorcising my identification with him. The final stop on my journey was to a semi-detached house in Catford where I spent a day with David Bradley, the actor who played Billy Casper in the film. He was now a middle-aged man, perhaps damaged by his experience of playing Billy Casper; he had never worked out a way of living his own life. He was politely bemused by my pilgrimage. I couldn't quite explain to him why I was there, nor what I wanted from him. I was shocked to hear him speak; he no longer had that beautiful Barnsley accent. His short-lived career as a stage actor had replaced that voice with a middle-class *tra-la-la*. We drank tea and he talked about backgammon tournaments. He would always be Billy Casper but I got the impression he no longer knew who he was. It troubled me that I'd bothered him and we left him there in his garden, listening to the birds. I asked each person I interviewed where they thought Billy Casper went after the book ended; every single person said, 'Nowhere. He'd have spent his whole life on the dole.'

On the edge of our housing estate was the wilderness. Here there were forests, caves, a lake where the golden knife-fish swam, and a black mountain where wars were fought between rival armies. The forests were made of stunted trees, weeds, spud plants and grass that towered above our heads, through which labyrinthine paths were trampled on commando raids to seize the enemy's weapons. The caves were down the transit camp manhole covers; we would crawl through shallow tunnels beneath stalactites of rusted pipes and electrical cables, over heaps of fly-tipping, scabbing our knees and elbows as we crawled, trying to get to the holy grail of looted treasure rumoured to be stashed in an abandoned fridge. The lake was a stinking bomb crater where we'd float ships of scaff planks and floorboards. When bulldozers and dumper trucks came and started levelling the transit camp we waded into the malarial water. With battered old Dulux tins we scooped fish out of the dirty pit as bulldozers filled the flooded hole with rubble. Recklessly I'd defy the bulldozers, holding up my paint pot full of tiddlers and goldfish. Fish like gold and silver flick knives with miraculous powers to protect the catcher.

Our war was a territorial dispute. To begin with, the ammunition was the fruit of flowering cherry trees. Then it was pea shooters. Then rocks. Running battles were fought for the possession of Black Mountain, the enormous mound of earth piled up by the bulldozers. Vietnam bled out of the television and into my violent imagination. My army was always the Viet Cong and we were ruthless in combat. We even practised rock-throwing at pop-bottle targets, shattering glass all over the gravel in front of the lock-up garages.

The Miller boy had a stash of oil-drum lids hidden in his coal bunker. They were shields for his army of Catholic school boys, stockpiled for the war against the new kids from the slums. I gathered a rebel force and we'd sneak down back alleys, over the backyard fences and into Miller's yard in the dark, stealing his oil-drum lids and sharpened mop handles and whooping like mercenaries and thieves. This was ecstasy, this was revolution. We were the new-kid scum and we had made our mark. We built a hideout of plastic sheeting, corrugated iron, asbestos sheets, planks from old barns and milk crates. We made guerrilla dens in lock-up garages, smashed-up bus shelters, flyover hideouts, the Nowhere Land of detritus where lives had been forgotten and discarded. There was nothing restorative about the landscapes I was walking through during this time or any other.

Billy Casper comes with me on my raids. Sometimes I go with a gang of lads to kill the cocky watchman. The old man sits there at his brazier, warming a tin of beans. We take table legs and cricket stumps and run across the building-site ditches, edging as close to him as we dare, quiet as we can be. One night I get so close to him I can reach out and poke him with my stick. He hunches there, smoking and spitting, slurping his stewed tea, poking the coals in the brazier. We always say we're going to kill him, but we always sneak away. One night he sees us skulking and throws burning timber at us; we run away terrified but laughing with the thrill.

We made folk devils out of complete innocents. An old woman who lived in a rundown cottage by the swing bridge became our Ginny Greenteeth – the Liverpool name for Jenny Greenteeth, or Wicked Jenny, the folklore river hag. Everybody knew she spent the nights beneath the water; she was a river witch, a canal hag who grabbed children and drowned them under the green pondweed. There were dead children on the bottom of the canal, weighted down and trapped inside the cages of shopping trolleys and pram frames. Ginny Greenteeth, the grindylow, had imprisoned them there in a larder that stretched halfway to Leeds.

The best of our folk devils was Fred Wilde the painter, who lived in a cottage by the dual carriageway and exhibited his abstract canvases in his front garden. His works were like migraines in paint, mad vortexes and mind-storms, aggressive geometries, psychotic weather. I remember him as a mad, wild-haired prophet. Once a year he exhibited his work at the local art society amongst the pastel Lake District landscapes and watercolours of flowers. Sometimes we'd climb into his garden and peek in through his windows. We couldn't frighten him because he was more frightening than any of us. Towards the end of his life he abandoned his Kandinsky rip-offs and settled down to paint quaint memories of cobbled streets and chimney sweeps: Lowryesque nostalgia. His house was demolished soon after he died, as if he were being exorcised for disrupting the dull conformity of the highway verges. Sadly, his work does not live on.

Down the canal by the strawberry farms a boy called Doyle gets off his bike, flips open a packet of cigarettes and passes one to me. I hold it in the V of my fingers, trying to look as if I know what I'm doing. He passes me the matches and I light up and suck hard, pulling the smoke into my lungs, feeling the instant dizzy hit. And then, using his teeth as a bottle opener, Doyle takes the top off a bottle of brown ale, gulps half of it down and passes it to me. I know a bit about drinking –

thanks to nana I've been drinking rum since I was three years old. As I sip the ale Doyle tells me the history of the dirt. 'All these fields, far as eyes can see, are deep in human shit. Night soil from Liverpool. One-hundred-and-fifty-years-old shite. The spuds you eat, the cabbages, the strawberries, are grown in human shite.' More than 150,000 tons of human waste was transported down the canal from Liverpool every year, I learnt, mixed with rubbish and coal-fire ash and dumped on the fields. The new town was built on Liverpool's sewage. Doyle gets back on his bike and cycles away, leaving me there with half a fag and the dregs left in the bottle. It's beautiful here in the watery, washed-out fens. The geese are flying over the fields. Sunlight glints off glasshouses, lights flashing like secret signals. Fat water voles – we used to think they were rats – drop into the canal and swim through the submerged wreckage of milk crate and pram. Sometimes I sing Billy Fury's 'Wondrous Place' and think about the beauty. *I found a place full of charms, a magic world in my baby's arms.*

The rough field with the abandoned buses is turned into a park, with swings and a slide and green grass for football. I miss the buses, miss climbing in amongst the manky paint pots and pretending to drive to Oklahoma. I miss the transit-camp ruins and the burnt barn. The sandy brook gets diverted into concrete pipes and more houses get built. It looks like anywhere else, and I have to go further to find my wilderness. Once I went on a voyage up the canal on the skinheads' polystyrene raft when they were away on some territorial skirmish. Bits of the raft, like globby white eggs, broke off and floated away on the canal murk. Once I followed a weather balloon that looked like a silvery UFO all the way up to some hills I'd often seen in the distance. I realised when I reached the hills that I was now *in the distance;* I'd reached the far away.

Even then I was a watcher. I would sit in the middle of potato fields and watch the enormous blue and grey sky that would pour into me and change my weather. I loved the geometric lines of the drainage ditches stretching into infinity. I loved that the canal – a graceful meander following the contour lines, a road made out of water – was made by men. One day I will go to Holland and I will know exactly where I am because the fields and fens of the Netherlands will look exactly like the fields of my marauding days. Sometimes the world seems to tilt in such a way that I can see the Irish Sea in the distance.

At night, I lie in bed and read *A Kestrel for a Knave*. I have begun to realise that my life is very different to Billy's; what we *do* have in common is a scrapheap education and a sense that we will have no say in our own futures. Billy will go down the pit or on the dole. I, too, will go on the dole as soon as I leave school, and then on to the Council. Billy's fate is written for him by his author, Barry Hines. But Hines had based it on the truth: boys like Billy were doomed. And so was his hawk.

> It had stopped raining. The clouds were breaking up and stars showed in the spaces between them. Billy stood for a while glancing up and down the City road, then he started to walk back the way he had come.
> When he arrived home there was no one in. He buried the hawk in the field just behind the shed; went in, and went to bed.

And that's the way the book ends; harsh, blunt, the plain facts. The hawk is dead and so are Billy's dreams. Downstairs in our living room 500,000 anti-war protesters are gathering outside the White House singing John Lennon's *Give Peace a Chance;* Apollo 12 is heading for the moon, and a Soviet submarine is colliding with an American submarine. I go to sleep imagining the end of all known things.

I wake up in the night and am still alive. None of us has been killed. There are no tanks on our streets, no guns. There is no napalm in the trees, no burning oaks. There are no mushroom clouds over the houses, no bodies reduced to ash. We have surrendered Black Mountain and the war is back inside the television. Once again in the quiet of night my mother tiptoes into the room I share with my sister Val and opens the bedroom curtains. Over the rooftops, all around the chimney pots, I watch the shadowplay of owls.

Transformer

The only good teacher I ever had was an art teacher who wore a kipper tie and found two treasures in a gutter. The first was a rain-soaked record, John Coltrane's *A Love Supreme*, which he played us one day in art class. Art was really an extension of detention, a place where the rejects and misfits ended up when they'd been kicked out of all the proper subjects. And there we sat, us scruffbags listening to this ecstatic, bebop violence, while the art teacher read to us from his second gutter treasure: a paperback copy of Franz Kafka's *Metamorphosis*, intoning like a beat poet over Coltrane's saxophone:

> As Gregor Samsa awoke one morning from uneasy dreams he found himself transformed in his bed into a gigantic insect.

It was startling, it was scary, but the whole experience had a cordite whiff of excitement. It was as if I'd woken from uneasy dreams, having passed through my own strange metamorphosis.

At the end of the lesson I had a look at the book, a Penguin Modern Classic with Max Ernst's painting of some bound and broken beast on the cover. I'd always been an avid, unschooled reader but this book had something thrillingly strange about it. Just holding it in my hands and skimming through its yellowed pages made me feel different. It was a bit like that rite of passage when I finally managed to bunk into *A Clockwork Orange* at the local fleapit and I felt illicit electricity surge through my veins. The universe had changed and so had I.

In those days there were at least a dozen bookshops in Liverpool and I used to spend my Saturdays and skiving days fingering the spines of books, looking for the stray dogs of literature. Some books were like animals: you could feel their hearts beating when you touched them. Finding one of those books was like discovering a new species. You'd want to keep it secret and watch how it moved and breathed before you showed it to your friends. Kafka wrote that a book should serve as an axe for the frozen sea beneath us; I felt the same way. I wanted to take risks with my imagination. Books were like drugs that could rearrange your mind.

One day, in a cardboard box in the comics shop on Moorfields, I found my own copy of *Metamorphosis*. Gregor Samsa was lurking there, surrounded by Marvel comic freaks – by Swamp Thing and the Incredible Hulk, Spider Man and Johnny Storm – but Gregor didn't need radioactive spiders or gamma-ray explosions to turn him into something other than himself; all he needed was a loathing for his job and a sleep of restless torment. I picked up the book and I could feel its pulse. It was alive.

Over a pint in the Masonic pub – probably plucking up the courage to buy a five quid of Lebanese Red – I began to read the book. I knew it was something I'd been searching for. At first, I didn't understand this powerful object in my hands, but I immediately knew I wanted it in my life. Not only that, I had the overpowering feeling that this was the way it had to be from now on – I had to live in a world of strange and wondrous things.

When I was a child I don't think it had ever really occurred to me that stories were written. It seemed to me they just somehow fell between the pages of books and waited to be discovered. Nor did I realise that some books were written in French or German and then translated into English, and that is how we were able to enter their worlds. I didn't learn a foreign language at

Franz Kafka
Metamorphosis
and Other Stories

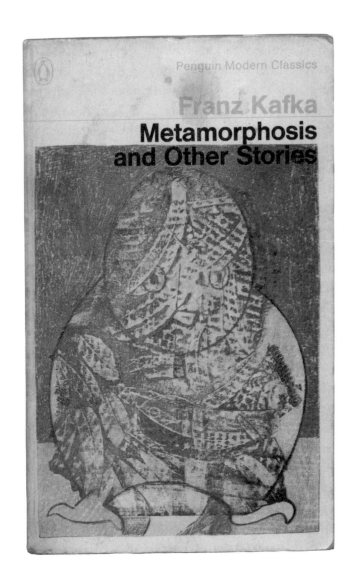

school. Until I was seventeen, when I hitched to Paris, I'd never even been abroad. I thought in English and saw the world in English. Round about this time I picked up a German-language edition of Kafka stories and I think – even though I couldn't read German – that seeing the words on the page in this strange language gave me a closer understanding of Kafka's intentions. I thought I could never really understand Kafka's stories because I couldn't get close enough to his thoughts. I didn't trust the translator. My Kafka stories were translated by Edwin and Willa Muir. How did I know they were telling the true story?

I had the feeling that there was a space between the German story and its English translation – an intangible, mysterious zone of misunderstanding. Kafka couldn't have known about this zone because he didn't know his stories would be translated. The only way to be certain of Kafka's intentions was to read his stories in the language they were written. But I was thrilled by the uncertainty. It made the books even stranger, made them more volatile and alien. A bookshop was a bestiary and the books on its shelves were like night-owls and salamanders, magical, strange, life-changing. When you find a new creature in the bestiary, and hold it in your hands, you don't know how its inner organs work but you can still feel the thrill of its heartbeat.

This was the beginning of a fascination with translation and of how one well-chosen – or mis-chosen – word meant that a man could be transformed into an insect in one translation of the book, and a bug in another. I started buying and comparing different translations of *Metamorphosis* and in one Gregor was a vermin and in another he was a cockroach. What did Kafka imagine?

Gregor Samsa is transformed – or translated – into an *Ungeziefer* – a creature with an untranslatable name. Maybe this was Kafka's intention: to make it difficult for us to identify the beast. Kafka refused to have an illustration of the creature on the book's cover. He wanted the reader to summon up their own image of Gregor's transformation.

Kafka named his hero something that can't be accurately translated. Perhaps, then, we readers of translations empathise with Samsa's plight in a different way. Samsa doesn't know what sort of creature he's been changed into and neither do we – nor should we. The translators are hesitant and uncertain about what to call the creature. He is unnameable ...

Edwin and Willa Muir's translations of Kafka have a tone of the mundane and the matter-of-fact about them. This adds to their oddness. It's as if Gregor, rather than turning into a monstrous beast, merely broke a butter dish – and his family, though irritated, are too polite to mention it. All the science-fiction books and fairy tales I'd read hadn't prepared me for this. Kafka was strange but his world was perfunctory and drab. I read somewhere that the Muirs weren't particularly fluent in German when they took on the translation job, which they did mainly because they needed the cash. Is Kafka drab and perfunctory because Edwin and Willa Muir's life was? I imagined them huddled at a kitchen table in their dressing gowns, ripping the books in half, scribbling and crossing out words with pencil stubs in a dimly lit apartment somewhere in Germany, ignoring the bills piling up on the doormat, making the world Kafkaesque for English readers, for teenage boys like me who were looking to be transformed.

I wasn't the only one. The Liverpool pubs and tea parlours were crowded out with thin young men in raincoats, reading their Kafka paperbacks. We were all immersed in a mass existential crisis in a world we defined – without really understanding what we meant – as 'Kafkaesque'. I found this confusing. Kafkaesque for me meant a nightmare realm where travelling salesmen could transform into monstrous cockroaches – I didn't see much evidence of this in Liverpool in the late 1970s. But when I moved on to *The Trial* and *The Castle* I think I began to understand, particularly as I was now working as a filing clerk in a Council office.

My mode of operation when I went to work each day was to make myself invisible. I invented a way of being present and absent. Through stillness, through lightness of footfall, I found I could get through the day without being noticed. My supervisor used to sit reading the Bible; *his* supervisor was an alcoholic, reeking of beer; *his* supervisor was a very important man who didn't seem to do any work. Nobody did any work and yet apparently this Council ran the city. They were Kafkaesque. I lived in a permanent state of anxiety, terrified that I would be found out, that I would become visible, dragged before the supervisors and punished for the crime of absence. It never happened. No one cared. I tried to read books by English writers but none of them had the strangeness that crawled out of Kafka and into my imagination. I was a young man in an overcoat who felt there was nothing more dangerous than a badly educated teenager with a pocketful of Josef K.

When I'm writing there are days when the words on the page seem too conventional; the story is too orderly, the characters aren't sufficiently bent or broken. I want there to be a touch of dissonance. I want the colours of the story to clash. I want the fabric of the story to be ripped and roughly stitched back together. In order to transform the material, I have to subvert or undermine the more conventional traits of my imagination. One of the ways I do this is to reach for Kafka. I've still got those tattered paperbacks from forty years ago and they're never far from my desk. Reading a few pages of *Metamorphosis* or *The Trial* tilts my imagination slightly off its axis. Kafka pushes me to imaginative extremes because I can't quite work out how he achieved his effects. I want my own writing to have an otherness about it, as if I've written the piece left-handed, or in a language I am struggling to understand.

I still mainly read books in translation and I can only manage the odd word in other languages. Recently, using a German dictionary, I made my own literal translation of the opening sentence: 'As Gregor Samsa one morning from a distempered dream awoke he found himself in his bed transformed into an enormous kind of unclean beast not fit for ritual sacrifice.'

I still don't really know what Kafka intended when he wrote his stories and I still don't completely trust his translators. There is something slightly Kafkaesque about the role of the translator as she negotiates a boundary between one language and another, between the writer and the reader. It's a kind of conjuring, a sleight of hand. We have to take it on trust that translators are responsible practitioners of magic.

Gregor Samsa is transformed. You could say he is *translated* from one state of being into another. When I read Kafka I wasn't just changed, I was translated.

Grandfather, Grey Rock

He was an old man when he went blind, so my grandad had already memorised the city. He could tell you which backyards had dairy cows and where to place an illegal bet. He looked like a proper old man – boots, navvy suit and flat cap – and there was an indentation the size of an old penny on the temple where, family folklore had it, he had had tiny glass ampules of radium injected to correct his failing vision. I imagined gamma rays and radioactive isotopes. I imagined him glowing in the dark.

I like to think the strange indentation on his skull was a kind of third eye through which he could see everything. He was a blind seer who could see the truth. And what he could see was erasure – the erasure of meaning. What he felt – what he saw – was empathy. My grandfather *was* the city and as the city was reduced so was he. The city's soul was dying and my grandfather's soul was turning to dust, like the brick and sandstone all around him. Yet he hung on to his kingdom – and his magnifying glass – for as long as he could, a symbol of resistance to blindness and destruction.

Today you can sit in Liverpool pubs beneath photographs of men long gone: dockers and carters, barrow boys and fruit sellers. I often search for my grandad on these saloon walls, amongst the flat-capped carters standing proudly by their horses, delivering sacks of hops to the brewery, flour to the mills, fruit to the Exchange. Once there were 20,000 horses on the streets of Liverpool and it's hard to imagine how the city must have sounded (and smelled). Once, I saw his ghost on Lodge Lane outside Maguire's Livery Stable, but it was a fleeting vision and he was gone before I could reach out to touch him. These men in the photographs are the true guardians of our city. Their dignity and bearing lends them an air of watchfulness. The sense of helplessness I often experience when I walk through Liverpool makes me feel close to what those men must have felt like as they said goodbye to their homes, pubs and market lanes, to the backyards where they used to stable horses.

The day I saw grandad's ghost outside the old livery stable I had been to the newsagent's to buy the Sunday paper. As I was paying, I was aware in my peripheral vision of a car pulling up at speed on the pavement, then of slamming doors and two men running into the shop. The men were wearing masks. I didn't take it seriously because the masks were clearly made from women's headscarves, and even though the men were waving sawn-off shotguns and shouting instructions it just seemed so ridiculous. But I was locked inside my body and couldn't move. One of the men climbed over the counter and forced the woman who ran the shop towards the cash register. She refused to open the till. He hit her with his gun, screaming at her, 'Open the fucking till!' The second masked man went to back him up and I kind of *dissolved* out of my body and walked towards the door, but when I looked back I was still there, frozen. I had walked out of my body. I went out into the street. And then, for some mad reason I went back into the shop. I'd like to think I was going to phone the police, but I think I felt I had to go back into the shop *because my body was still in there.* I walked back into my body, the men screaming and swearing at me, and then one of them – in a mask of vivid marigolds – made me lie down on the floor and put a gun to my head. Lying down on the floor, I realised, quite calmly, that I was going to die. I was still holding *The Observer*.

And then it was over, as quick as it had begun. The men had smashed the till open and were running out with the takings, jumping into the stolen car, and driving away with The Orb's *Little Fluffy Clouds* blasting out of the car CD player, as if they were soundtracking their own getaway with someone else's taste in music. Everything was distorted, reverberating. I felt like I was weighed down with cement at the bottom of a flooded building, passively submitting to oblivion. And yet I wasn't dead, or even wounded. When the police came they insisted the men were carrying lengths of copper piping until they checked the CCTV footage and admitted, yes, they were carrying guns. And then, as the cops were driving me home, I looked out of the rear window of the van and saw my grandad – flat cap, navvy suit, waistcoat, boots, a dead man looking at me, standing in the shop doorway beneath a sandstone carving of a horse.

I needed to find a way of containing all this. If I didn't believe in ghosts, why had I just seen one? Why was it my grandad? It must have been connected with the old livery stables. Perhaps he'd stabled horses there and had returned through a portal instigated by my trauma. I decided to go on a walk to looking for him. My thinking was, if I can find my grandad I can heal the trauma. And it *was* trauma. For months, I found it difficult to walk the city streets; I would break out in a sweat if I heard a car pulling up behind me. I couldn't go back inside the newsagent's. Whenever I saw two young men together I imagined they were the robbers. So I walked from Lodge Lane to Grey Rock Street, searching for grandad's ghost.

In 1962 Henri Cartier-Bresson came to Liverpool and took photographs outside the Lodge Lane washhouse; a tangle of prams and pushchairs parked up on Grierson Street; a headscarved woman pushing a laundry bundle up the street on a home-made trolley; a small girl presumably guarding the prams for a threepenny bit. The woman walks into the photograph, head bowed, watching her bundle. She doesn't want to make eye contact with us, but further down the street a woman stares right into the lens of Cartier-Bresson's Leica, and through that, into our eyes. The young man on the bike, the kid on the home-made 'steery' go-cart are frozen in time. Elsewhere in the city, Cartier-Bresson finds three small girls in winter coats and white ankle socks hurrying past a derelict lock-up, by the ruins of an old townhouse, half obliterated by mist. It's beautiful and poignant and moves me in a way akin to grief.

Cartier-Bresson walked these streets. I picture him wearing a Harris Tweed overcoat, woollen scarf and black trilby; his face is half-man, half-Leica and the eye I can see is closed behind his tortoiseshell specs. His leather-soled shoes tap on the cobbles as his head turns, almost imperceptibly, scanning the streets for images. He looks like a man lost in a ruined city, like a man walking through the aftermath of war. And without her even noticing, he captures the woman in the headscarf. When I lived on Lodge Lane in the 1990s, the place looked more or less the same: women in headscarves, kids playing among the debris, deprivation, hardship, stoic resilience. On my walk to Grey Rock Street, having no camera, I took mental photographs of similar women and children on the street where the washhouse used to be – sideways glance, surreptitious click of my eyelids. I see buildings that are haunted by other people's grandparents. I let the memories pass into me. I walk back through the years.

One day in the 1960s, I went to Grey Rock Street with my dad not long after grandad and nana had been relocated to a block of low-rise flats in Knotty Ash. This is what my last visit to the house looks like: there are corrugated sheets on the windows and front door and the house is the last one standing. My dad and I stand on the pavement. 'This is the same pavement where I once saw Uncle Ted pouring a kettle of boiling water down a crack between the flagstones and laughing as thousands upon thousands of ants came hurtling out in a mass evacuation. I remember being horrified, watching ants being boiled *alive*.' We stand there on the pavement and then my dad tests the metal sheet that blocks up the front door. He pulls the tin away, bends the bottom corner over, just enough for us to crawl inside, and once inside we stand there in the dark

lobby, waiting for our eyes to adjust to the gloom. And then we go upstairs. In the bedroom that my dad used to share with his three brothers, he kneels down on the floor and digs a spoon into a gap between the floorboards. He prises a section of floorboard loose and pulls it free. Then he puts his hand into the gap beneath the floor and rummages around. Concentrating, frowning, searching. And then he smiles – he takes out a biscuit tin and puts it gently down on the floorboards, opens the lid and inside there is a dirty rag bundle, which is really disappointing to me. But my dad unwraps the bundle like a magician and the audience of one child is hushed. Inside the bundle, oh such treasures! Water pistol, fountain pen, shrapnel, shell-case, penknife, photograph of the dog he had when he was young, beer-bottle marbles. We look at the objects, hold them up to the light in wonder. Then he wraps the treasure back in the rag and carries the tin downstairs. For the last time we look around the kitchen, the parlour, the house where he was born. This is where he used to climb through the skylight during the Blitz and lie down on the rooftop, watching the Luftwaffe flying over, watching the docks in flames. This is where nana, Queen of Red Rock Street, sat at the kitchen table, spooning sugar into glasses of lemonade to take away the fizz. This is where I imagined the river waters rising up from the cellar and carrying grandad and nana away. This is the house that will soon cease to exist. All of it is imagination, myth, a haunted museum of memory.

In Kensington, another museum. Grandma's house was always dark: the gloom of oak-panelled rooms, of mahogany furniture and soot. When grandad Albert was alive he was the central presence in the room they called the kitchen – the room between the back kitchen and the front parlour where the fire burnt and the radiogram played old songs. Albert would sit in the chair near the fire wearing a dark suit and highly polished boots. He was made of papery skin and if you pressed his fingertips they would compress in such a way that they were concave instead of convex, as if he were slightly deflated. He was a very patient man who would let you sit on his knee, take his handkerchief out of his breast pocket and polish his bald head. He smelled of pipe tobacco and warm leather – smelled the same as his tobacco pouch – and he was altogether comforting and gentle and kind. Like everyone else in our family he seemed to be dying a slow and stoic death, always spitting phlegm into ripped-up pieces of the *Liverpool Echo*, screwing the paper into balls and throwing them into the coals where they would sizzle and smell of ruined lungs. I think he was slowly being killed by Ogden's pipe tobacco and the darkness that seeped into him from the shadows of the room. When grandad Albert died he was *still* the central presence in the room because his leather and tobacco smell lingered in the chair beside the fire where he used to sit and spit.

Grandma did the flowers at St Luke's. The church was as dark as her house, a whisper-palace where no one ever raised their voice. If grandad was made of leather, gabardine, tobacco and spit then grandma was made of daffodils, furniture polish and prayer books.

And laughter, often or always. There are photographs of them when they were young, grandma dressed like a school ma'am and grandad like Will Hay. There are memories of Christmas time, where the wind-up gramophone is scratching out 'The Laughing Policeman' or 'How Much is That Doggy in the Window', and everyone is singing along like they were doing a turn on a music-hall stage.

After grandma died, my mum and I went to pack up her house. She was gone but she was still there; you could sense her presence in the furniture, in the tea caddy, in the enamel bowl in the Belfast sink. I played a few notes on the piano in the parlour and touched the jet-black statuettes of Roman gods on the mantelpiece. And then we went upstairs. Grandma's presence in the front bedroom was overwhelming. The pink candlewick bedspread was neatly folded back, the feather pillows plumped. My mum ran a duster over the walnut dressing table – the one I used to love for the cut whorls in the grain. She began to pack things into boxes, starting with the tortoiseshell dressing-table set. I watched her. She picked up a round lidded pot and held it in her hands, shaking slightly. She dipped her finger into the opening in the pot lid and then pulled out a coil of grandma's hair. As she twirled her finger, more and more hair came spooling out. To begin with it was old-lady grey, then it became darker, becoming brownish, becoming reddish, becoming auburn, becoming a young woman's glorious curls. Every night before she went to bed my grandma had brushed her hair, and then she'd removed the loose hairs from the brush and pressed them into the tortoiseshell bowl. We were looking at a lifetime, an autobiography told in coils of hair.

In my memory, I can smell the hair burning. I don't know if we *did* burn grandma's hair, but I can still smell the sulfurous, charcoal smell. Perhaps I've made a ritual to commemorate her bedtime routine: putting on her hand-embroidered nightdress, unpinning her hair and letting it fall over her shoulders, slipping into the bed she once shared with my grandfather.

Now I have several locks of my daughter's hair, tucked in between books or weighted with pebbles on a shelf. To me they are sacred objects, talismans. Thy are possessed with meaning and memory.

I have dreams of being stranded in flooded buildings, unable to climb down the fire escape to rescue my drowning daughter. I get out of bed and go on a walk to try to find some peace. In those dreams I am blind like my grandfather. Did he wake up thinking 'I'm not blind, it's just a dream'?

In my radio piece, *Red Rock, Grey Rock* I tried to create a seance – a place where I could contact the dead using snatches of hymns sung by my nana, mental images of chests of drawers full of radio and television valves, the mad possibility that the aurora borealis *might* appear over the rooftops of Liverpool, the ghostly apparition outside the newsagent's, the fear I felt when I thought the men with guns might kill me, the attempts I made to 'see' the world through a blind man's eyes. In *Red Rock, Grey Rock* grandad tells us how his working life ended:

Last job I ever did was for an undertaker … a haulage job taking broken coffins from a graveyard that was no longer used … I had to load the wagon up with bodies and drive them out to a cemetery on the edge of the city … I'd gone from hauling coal and oats and beer barrels to driving the dead to hell … And when the job was over … it must have taken a week … I never got paid … the undertaker was bankrupt … and I went under too … I sat there at the kitchen table trying to do the sums … but I couldn't magic money and we needed jam and bread … I started selling off … my dad said these motors were only going to be a fad … the world would see sense and horses'd win the day … he was wrong … I sold the coal round to Davie Hulme and let the stables go to blokes with motors … it was all over. Might as well have gone to hell with all the corpses.

My grandfather had a map inside his heart of the city he had lived in all his life. He couldn't hear the bulldozers, couldn't see the houses falling. He would walk along the desolate wasteland streets, his inner compass guiding him past the ghosts of vanished terraced houses, corner shops, alehouses, the butcher's and the baker's. There was nothing to the left, nothing to the right, nothing on any of the four horizons except for debris and rubble. The cobbled streets still framed the emptiness, but there was no one left to walk through the frames, no photographer to capture the city as it once was. Just grandad walking through a city which is no longer there.

Stalking Time for the Moon Boys

Even when I grew older it was useful to be able to make myself invisible – especially when the boot boys came to town. The car park outside the Country Club was a gathering ground for local gangs, most of whom I knew. Even Spacey Moon, the psychopath who used to throw kids in the canal, gave me the benefit of the doubt; but I was still nervous of walking past them after dark in case they mistook me for a blow-in and gave me a battering around the back of the nightclub by the bins. It wasn't the local gangs that bothered me, it was the *proper skinheads* from Kirkby who would come to town once a week to terrorise the innocent or attend some prearranged grudge battle, the fulfilment of a violent obligation. People said they came in stolen cars with weapons in the boot. They were Viking raiders driving down the country lanes, immaculately dressed in Flemings jeans and Airwair.

I'm sixteen, flunked out of school. I've just got a job in a vegetable-packing warehouse further up the canal towards the Moss, where the world starts to look like Holland – wide and horizontal with skies bigger than the land. I work with a man who steals knives and stashes them in the lining of his car coat. During tea breaks he lifts weights with crates full of spuds and onions, and on Friday lunchtimes after a few pints in the canalside pub he challenges me to a fight, every Friday without fail. I never fight him – I've seen the knives – but sometimes I go to the pub and watch him drinking. Sinking five pints, six pints, drooling over the barmaid, slumped there in his overalls covered in mud from wet vegetables. He rattles like a cutlery drawer, or a weapons dump on legs. He gets so pissed he can hardly walk back to the packing warehouse. I follow him, watch him pissing in the ditch, singing to himself as he staggers. His hands are covered in bandages and sticking plasters from accidents on the packing line. No one stops him, everyone's frightened. *Fight me. Fight me!* He squares up to me. I keep my head down and get on with my job of stacking crates full of onions, nine across, nine high, strap them with rubber belts, move them into the refrigerated room. One day he sees me stealing tomatoes to take home to my mum and he snitches on me to the boss, who docks my wages. I imagine he's going to kill me. In the van that drops us back in town he sits there, surrounded by knives. It occurs to me that he's some kind of malevolent spirit, a Golem made of mud and weapons. I think he got the sack for some kind of psychotic episode; I watched him in the town centre, knives in both hands, laughing, stabbing tyres.

It's sometime in the early 1970s and all I care about is art, music and paperbacks. The school I have just left is a mediocre Secondary Modern where no one even noticed I existed. The only thing I could do was draw and paint, and so in the last two years of school that's more or less all I did. Over and over I'd daub dark colours onto sheets of wallpaper trying to replicate the enormous skies that hung in winter over the fens and ditches of my chosen territory. I'd rub charcoal into the pigment with my thumbs. I'd spit onto the paper trying to make bad weather. At the end of a lesson I'd hang the painting up to dry and next time I had a lesson I'd take it down and paint over it again and again, building up the sky in layers of smear and daub and smudge and spit. I could never get it right. I'd go down the canal and look at the sky for ages. Sometimes I'd go with a boy called Hayes and sit next to him while he fished for perch and roach near the dual carriageway bridge. Hayes had actually learnt a fragment of Ted Hughes's *Pike:*

Pike, three inches long, perfect
Pike in all parts, green tigering the gold.
Killers from the egg: the malevolent aged grin.
They dance on the surface among the flies.
Or move, stunned by their own grandeur
Over a bed of emerald, silhouette
Of submarine delicacy and horror ...

And Hayes would point into the shadows beneath the bridge where a pike of local legend lurked, *like a fucking assassin,* as he liked to say. So here was poetry. Ted Hughes's *Crow* took its place on my shelf, up there next to *Robinson Crusoe, Huckleberry Finn* and *A Child's Garden of Verses.* They didn't teach me anything at school so I began to teach myself. I remade myself out of Picador paperbacks and Penguin Modern Classics. I'd go to Philip, Son and Nephew and spend my birthday money on sable paint brushes and paperbacks. This wondrous place full of books and paint was paradise. Here I'd browse through Henry Miller's *Tropic of Cancer,* trying to pluck up the nerve to buy it. I wanted to live at the Villa Borghese. I'd never read anything like it; I didn't even know stories like this were possible. I dreamed of Paris, of romantic squalor:

There is not a crumb of dirt anywhere, nor a chair misplaced. We are all alone here and we are dead. Last night Boris discovered that he was lousy. I had to shave his armpits and even then, the itching did not stop. How can one get lousy in a beautiful place like this? But no matter. We might never have known each other so intimately, Boris and I, had it not been for the lice.

These are some of the things that happen during my school days: Neil Armstrong and Buzz Aldrin are walking on the moon, gazing on magnificent desolation; a girl in my class disappears for three days and people say she is living on the landfill site (I dream of her amidst the gulls, the lost queen of the dump in mists of methane); on television American planes bomb Cambodia; in the night a boy called Frank is killed on the dual carriageway and boys in school whisper of how his body was carried away in bin bags; The Beatles split up, which makes my mother sad; the schoolboy all the girls loved is blinded in Balls Wood with an arrow made from a bamboo stick and six-inch nail; my sister Val listens to Tamla Motown 45s in her bedroom, practising her dance moves as Smokey Robinson sings; Ashby, the Geography teacher, flexes his cane until it splinters and looks like a cat o' nine tails. A boy who stole a girl's leather trench coat tries to gas himself in the chemistry lab. (Because he's cut the coat up to make a bomber jacket he can't take up the headmaster's offer to return it anonymously, 'no questions asked'.) The Green Jackets are coming; the word is out, and the entire school is sent home because the GJs have been known to leave kids for dead in school playgrounds all over the north. There's no such gang but everyone believes in them. They bring danger to the suburbs and I want them to exist.

I go walking through the fields with a girl called Carol. People think she's my girlfriend, but we never kiss, never once hold hands.

On Friday nights we go to the Albany cinema; more like an enormous prefab than a palace of dreams, but it's the cinema where I start to watch 'grown-up' films. One afternoon I'm watching *Bedknobs and Broomsticks* with my parents; the next night I'm watching *Straw Dogs* with Carol. When I remember those cinema trips, images come to me of *Harold and Maude*, *Black Beauty*, *Straw Dogs* and *Dumbo*, a Disney elephant flying through Peckinpah carnage.

We watch *A Clockwork Orange* and the world tilts even further off its axis. One night a gang of suedeheads assemble in the car park and transform into droogs. They've painted their denim jeans white and they're wearing bowler hats and false lashes on their right eyes. During one Friday-night screening, there are policemen standing in a line behind the back row. Just in front of them, in hushed defiance, boys and girls are touching each other. The town starts to feel dangerous and exciting. Violent young men are wearing mascara. In NEMS in the shopping centre we get our first sighting of Ziggy Stardust. We stand there, gazing at the sleeve for ages, desiring this creature from the stars. My sister Val buys me the record for Christmas and I sit in my bedroom listening to its mutant songs over and over. I read the lyrics, trying to decipher hidden messages. I gaze at David Bowie on the sleeve and he is beautiful. Ziggy Stardust feels like the brother of Alex from *A Clockwork Orange*. I buy Anthony Burgess' book in Philip, Son and Nephew. I learn to *govoreet* Nadsat. The words *droog* and *tolchock*, *bitva* and *bratchny* become part of my vocabulary. I feel like a *chelloveck* and the world is *choodessny*.

I begin to realise these suburban towns – the dormitory, the overspill – are incredibly strange. Grown-up parties in neighbours' houses could have been written by Jacqueline Susann. Men are kissing women who are not their wives. Gangs of boys steal nail varnish from Woolworth's and walk in Kubrick and Peckinpah slow-motion. A crew of skinheads sail down the cut on a polystyrene raft, dressed like Malcom McDowell: it all seems eminently plausible. Boys who used to buy Tamla Motown 45s on the first day of release are now buying Lou Reed and wearing Oxford bags and platform shoes. At a church fete I watch men smashing a piano to smithereens with sledgehammers. The piano moans and groans and dies like a slaughtered beast. The men's vests are stained with sweat, and mums I know are visibly aroused.

Inspired by the sleeve of Syd Barrett's *The Madcap Laughs,* Hoppy is painting his floorboards with orange and purple stripes while his parents are on holiday in Prestatyn. Hoppy likes to smoke roll-ups – I think he likes to imagine they're spliffs – and talk about 'the Floyd'. I don't know anything about Pink Floyd apart from being aware they're the sort of band the A-Level kids are into. But Syd is different. He appeals to the wastrel in me, the bad poet, the would-be dissolute. Boys like Hoppy are my polytechnic. For some reason, he has an oscilloscope and we watch waveform signals on its screen. We call ourselves cosmonauts. Unknown to me at this time there are other boys like me in the Liverpool suburbs who are looking for ways to make their world strange. On June 10 1973, I go to watch David Bowie morph into Ziggy Stardust at the Liverpool Empire. The music is transcendent and exhilarating, and the theatre is like a carnival reeking of sweat and lust. Everybody wants to touch Ziggy Stardust, everybody thinks he is looking into their eyes. It is an erotic ceremony, an electric circus of desire.

My dad comes home telling us he had to burn a warehouse full of comics in the printing factory. I picture him on the night-shift, printers' ink on his rough hands, wandering through the warehouse fingering thousands of comics as if saying goodbye before they are set on fire. A sadness weighs on his shoulders as he sits in the parlour confessing that he'd taken one comic, the first ever *Eagle* with the spaceship Anastasia in the centrefold. We read it at supper time. Somewhere on Mercury, Dan Dare is watching us through incinerator flames.

Last week at school I almost kissed a girl and I don't know what to do with the desire. Her name is Nuala. Someone tells me she lives on a smallholding in a place called Melling, and one night I go looking for her house, just so that I can know where she belongs. Down along the ditches, running in the dark, I snag my jacket on a barbed-wire fence and cut my arm, all in pursuit of an imagined kiss. Over by the asylum I can see the glass house, and imagine her waiting there, amongst the oil drums and turpentine and weeds, scratching our names into dirt-streaked panes of glass. Soon, the moon will pass overhead and shine on her pale skin. And I know that when I get there there'll be love tokens hanging, festooned on withered roses: that choker she wears to school discos, her underwear, a plastic ring she got from a bubblegum machine. I'll arrive as the moonbeam hits the broken panes of glass and she'll be gone, but I'll sleep in the glasshouse anyway, aching. I'll skive off school, drink a can of shite, steal potatoes, build roll-ups with one hand. I'll stand in the dirt where she'd been waiting, while one by one the panes of glass fall through me to the ground.

Hoppy is carrying the wrong LP sleeve under his arm. If it

was Aladdin Sane he'd be okay, but for some typically eccentric reason he's flaunting a Mahavishnu Orchestra album. On the dual carriageway bridge, on his way to the Baptist church youth club, Hoppy is ambushed by Spacey Moon and his glammed-up boot boys. I watch as they hurl him down the embankment, watch as *The Inner Mountain Flame* flies through the air and then skids along the canal. They don't lay a finger on me. For some reason, I get through these scrapes and skirmishes. I don't know why, but I'm immune to the violence on the streets.

And when it's Easter time the travelling fair comes to town, pitching up on the wasteland next to the youth club. You can hear the music and screaming from miles away and kids from all over town descend on the rough field to flirt and fight and ride the waltzers and dodgems. You can hear the whine of Lambrettas as The Cloud ride in formation down the dual carriageway – these are the older brothers of the boot boys, immaculate creatures with sharpened steel combs in their back pockets. And when they park up the girls crowd around them, stroking their scooters as if they were beasts. My sister Val and I are barred from going to the fairground, but we go anyway. I love the sound of the generator and the smells of fried onions and candy floss mixed with the smell of horseshit rising from trampled ground. As The Cloud start rucking with the local boys to the soundtrack of Cockney Rebel's *Mr Soft*, I see my dad walking slowly, purposefully through the mayhem, straight towards me with a look of fury on his face. I make myself invisible. He walks right through me, doesn't see me. He goes straight up to Val, who is watching the fight from the waltzers.

Steel-toed boots connect with bone, steel combs slice skin. My dad takes Val by the shoulder and guides her through the carnage. As they stride past, Val turns to me and mimes *Fuck you!* I am shaking with fear. I am invisible. It is stalking time for the moon boys and I watch unseen from the shadows.

In the last month at school they threaten to expel me for not wearing a uniform. I get sent home with a letter from the deputy headmaster telling my parents if I don't return to school dressed appropriately they'll be receiving another letter telling them my education has been terminated. It's been terminated anyway because it's patently obvious I'm not going to achieve anything. I'm wearing hand-me-down suedehead clothes that belonged to one of my cousins: two-tone petrol-blue parallel trousers, button-down Ben Sherman shirt with a pink fleck, and tasselled golf shoes. I want to tell them to fuck off, but my mum wants to make a point. She rises to the challenge and makes me a uniform from bits of my sister's (different school, different colour). Burns takes one look at me and signs me off with a sneer of contempt and my letter of release. I leave the school for good. By the swings in the park, boys who've been expelled are setting their uniforms on fire. One whips his burning tie around his head; the ashes float off towards the bowling green.

In school, we weren't allowed to live in our own universes. We were crushed by conformity. When I left, I took *A Clockwork Orange* and *Ziggy Stardust* as operating manuals for disobedience. When I handed over money for *Hunky Dory*, took it home and pored over the lyrics, I knew I'd been transported. *It was stalking time for moon boys* in this north Liverpool town, and the drab was painted in Day-Glo. And once I discovered that I could transform the world using my imagination I felt – I *knew* – there was nothing they could do to extradite me. I and all the other moon boys and moon girls were beyond their reach. We spoke in a secret code. A language for freaks and misfits – whether that was David Bowie and Mick Ronson on Top of the Pops, the glossary of Nadsat words at the back of a Penguin paperback, the sound of Wendy Carlos's version of *Ode to Joy* reverberating through a fleapit cinema's speakers, or the endless playing of vinyl records in our bedrooms, trying to decipher the meaning of phrases such as 'jamming good with Weird and Gillie' or 'screwed-up eyes and screwed-down hairdo like some cat from Japan'. These were nonsense words but they popped and fizzed like fireworks; they were signals from a parallel suburb far away, a science fiction universe right at the end of our street.

From the top of Poverty Lane bridge, I could see Liverpool's cathedrals. I want to go there. I want to live there. Even though I love the fields and the cut and the straight-line ditches, I don't want to be in this town. Not for the first time I sink into depression. I descend into depths murkier than the bomb-crater ponds. I retreat into bed and books and signing-on the dole once a fortnight. When I do manage to drag myself out of bed it's to go walking slowly down the canal, looking at water bugs, sticklebacks, assassin pike beneath the bridge. It takes me forever, my lethargy dragging me down, but I walk along the towpath and sit in the ruins of an old abbey. It's peaceful here in the daytime; at night time drunks from the nearby pub come here for a shag. But here I am, alone in the ruins, finding a momentary peace.

One evening at dusk I sneak into a fenced-off patch of wasteland down along the railway track. I take off my boots and socks and walk through the swampy moss. Then I take off all my clothes and lie on the trunk of a fallen tree, moss and lichen pressing into my body. I lie there on the edge of sleep, feeling as if I've undressed out of my depression, feeling quiet-minded and content. In the woods, I find an un-sprung animal snare and even though I'm appalled by this vicious contraption I find it strangely exciting. It means that there are poachers hereabouts. It means there are places on the edge of my town that are impossible to control. This is *the other*, as strange as anything in *The Owl Service*; a place of uncanny atmospheres, an unmapped realm.

Ziggy Stardust, slightly warped on the Dansette. The girl I kissed down the country lane is dancing with a girl who looks just like her – feather cut, penny-round collar, Oxford bags, platform shoes. I watch from the safety of the youth-club doorway. It's Friday night and the droogs are lining the walls, watching the pretty girls, watching the other boys, watching themselves in the strobe and ultraviolet dark. I don't go in. I never kiss the girl from the country lane again. I turn around and walk slowly home, through the gangs in the country-club car park. *I am invisible.*

The Observer's Book of Vandalism

A man floats down the River Dee in a hessian sack, bobbing along on the current, out into the estuary. This man's name is Gwion, and he has been regurgitated into the sack by a hunchbacked hag named Ceridwen. When Gwion met the hag she was boiling a concoction of charm-herbs – she intended to anoint her son Morfran with three drops of the brew, investing him with powerful wisdom. But it all went a bit haywire and three drops of the potion splashed on Gwion, much to the hag's fury. He fled the angry hag, transforming himself into a fish and then a crow to deceive Ceridwen. Each time Gwion changed form, however, Ceridwen made herself into a predator of that creature. Gwion was exhausted by the pursuit and made the mistake of becoming a grain of wheat, which the hag simply swallowed. With Gwion in her belly, Ceridwen transformed herself from hag to river goddess and regurgitated him in a human form, then tied him in a sack and dumped him in the water – which is where we join him, bobbing along the estuary, until he is caught by a salmon fisherman and instantly recognised and worshipped as the sun god returning.

Now, a few details might have gone awry in my telling of it here, but this is as close as I can get, a kind of Punk-Mabinogion, which I tell to Pearl and my partner Amy one evening, early in the year, standing on the sewage-polluted sands of Thurstaston beach. As I do my best to impress upon them that *this is where it happened,* suddenly the pale, late-afternoon light switches to full-on Pink Floyd light show and the estuary opens up and ruptures the sky, creating a gaping hole of bright energy, vast and peaceful and exhilarating all at once, a chemical fusion of acid yellows and pinks and blues and silvers, some of it as dazzling as chrome, some of it as visionary as a Turner painting, daubs and streaks and openings and closures of religious intensity. The strollers and dog-walkers, the kite-flyers and litter-pickers come to a standstill, transfixed by the great display. It's like our own aurora borealis.

We come here four times a year, in winter, spring, summer and autumn. We come when we're feeling a bit damaged and exhausted with our lives and the hurtling rollercoaster of days. I am carrying unidentifiable minerals (unmentioned in my *Observer's Book of Geology*) in my pocket, treasure stones I can touch, perhaps for luck, perhaps just for the tactile pleasure. I like to pretend they are fragments of fallen stars. We come here from Liverpool to experience our own transformation. We come here because it's not like anywhere else. The path that drops down from the road to the shore is a portal, emerging into a vast, echoing sky. We exist in the absolute moment here, in a place where all the memories that follow us around can't reach. It is a place separate from memory-chaos, seemingly surrounded by some elemental force field. We wear different skin here. Our souls are shimmering.

I try to identify birds. In midwinter, there must be 10,000 dunlin and knot here; in autumn, the same number of shelduck. At low tide on the marsh banks between here and Connah's Quay on the Welsh coast some 100,000 birds gather: dunlin, ringed plover, sanderling, whimbrel, oystercatchers, godwits, curlew, redshank, sand martin, and up the river at Parkgate there are avocets and egrets. When the tide comes in and covers the mud an echoing panic and commotion of displacement ensues. The knot and dunlin shift up to the shore. We walk among the crowds of restless birds. Above our heads the occasional peregrine or kestrel passes. All this activity adds a nervousness to the scene, unsettling the atmosphere.

I used to come here when I was a child with a neighbour whose name I can't recall. I had been to Malham Cove in Yorkshire on a rare school trip and come back with slabs of limestone etched with fossilised creatures, which I later found out were crinoids at least 250 million years old. I kept the rocks on my bedroom window shelf with a table lamp shining down on them so I could see into their universes. For my fourteenth birthday I was given *The Observer's Book of Geology* and a Hamlyn guide to fossils; I gave myself a scrappy education in the wonders of echinoids and foraminifera. On a family holiday in Dorset I collected ammonites and lumps of iron pyrites or 'fool's gold'. I thought my most treasured piece was a shark's tooth but it turned out to be a belemnite, similar to a squid. Sometimes I would just hold it, cupped in the palm of my hand. I found this ancient creature by splitting open a rock, like opening a stone purse and finding a message from the depths of space. It made no immediate sense to me, but it was incredibly powerful.

The cliffs here at Thurstaston are glacial deposits left 17,000 years ago. They're constantly eroding, eaten away when storms batter the cliffs with heavy waves. The cliff-mud oozes and spews, its wet skin shines in the sunlight, it is somehow *obscene*, like exposed bodies or shit.

In 2013 a cliff collapse caused by heavy seas exposed the ruins of a farm building, which fell down to the shore. Jammed into the cliffs there are countless glacial erratics – pieces of sandstone, granite, quartz crystal, and huge boulders suspended ten or twenty feet above our heads, transported here by ice from Scotland and across the Irish Sea. Calcite, hematite, mica, pyrite and zircon are often found here; the geology of Britain in the volatile mud of a River Dee. Each time we come here, new secrets have been exposed. Sometimes we find fossils on the shore. Pearl fills her pockets with crystals, takes them home and washes them in the sink, just as I did when I was child.

In bad weather, there are spectacular collapses; huge sections of sodden earth break off and fall down to the shore, exposing broken sewage pipes, guttering, rusted metal. When we walk along the shore we are stepping over house bricks, broken paving stones, breezeblocks, gas canisters, pieces of machinery and wrecked boats. We see thousands and thousands of tiny crabs scuttling across the gritty sand, so many that it's impossible to walk without crushing them beneath your boots. Always, there is the shifting, changing light. You can tell the time by the clock-hands of sunbeams spanning the bay.

My dad took me to a neighbour's house and he showed me his collection of stones, displayed on shelves in a glass extension, row upon row of minerals, slabs of veined marble, trilobite and vertebrae-embedded limestone. Round about this time I think I had some kind of nervous breakdown. I remember standing at the top of the railway bridge and watching a crop duster flying over the fields. I remember willing it to drop its invisible cloud on me. I remember wishing for the bee-swarm to return and cover me in insects. I remember retreating into a world of chaotic imagination made out of Jennings and Darbishire books, an obsession with sable paintbrushes, *The Owl Service*, William Blake, the Silver Surfer, Vincent Van Gogh's paintings of sunsets, Ursula Le Guin. I remember obsessively walking for miles, muttering out loud, worrying, frightened, terribly lonely and yet wanting to be alone, wanting to feel lonely. I was walking through a chaos of creatures and children's books and obsession with strange poetry and stars. With my paper-round money I bought the Observer's books of wild flowers, pond life, insects, trees and shrubs, astronomy, freshwater fishes, butterflies, caterpillars. My fossil and rock collection grew, my bedroom became a museum of Paleozoic wonders.

It *sounds* different here. The air has a particular acoustic property, its own sonic atmosphere. Voices and the call of birds come to you as if contained in some kind of epic sound-capsule. Sometimes there is a held-breath wonder, a crystal-clear clarity, a fleeting moment of precision. Most of the time there is a *thickness*, as if the world has been drugged. It sounds like it has snowed in the night, even when it's a summer's day. Smudged sound. A dream within an absence. I have had hallucinations here, caused by the weight of sound and space.

If I were going to impose a soundtrack on this place it would be Mercury Rev's album *Deserter's Songs*. The record summons up images of hallucinatory skies, glow-worms, fireflies, glimmering fires in strange landscapes, astronomical awe and the bittersweet melancholy of sunset sadness. When I had labyrinthitis it felt like these songs. I can hear it in my head sometimes as I gaze into the heat-shimmer out towards the distant sea. But the shore has its own orchestra and has no need of such an imposition.

You can dig into the cliff's flesh with your fingers and pull out quartz crystals and what might be gypsum. It's like plunging your hands into an animal. When I came here as a child with our neighbour, we tapped at the cliffs with our geologists' hammers and filled a shoebox with pieces of ancient history. Other boys had looted birds' eggs; I had pieces of limestone covered with the stone ghosts of sea creatures.

It occurs to me that these treasure hunts and excavations are similar to my diggings into memory; the unearthing and revealing of lost history, buried memory, excavated erratics. Even when I wasn't writing stories down I was digging them out of the earth, holding them in my hands, trying to make a connection with their meanings. When my mother died, I inherited a silver matchbox she had had since she was a child. It had belonged in turn to her grandfather, a beautiful relic engraved with coiled ferns. Open the hinged lid and you will find inside eleven tiny objects: two ivory elephants; a photograph of my mum's mother; a silver charm-bracelet donkey; a golden heart-shaped locket; a Maltese cross collar stud; a Canadian George IV nickel; the tally for her dog Ted, made out of a Victorian sixpence; a lucky black cat from a Christmas cracker; a blue, transparent fruit from a child's necklace. These were her treasures, safely tucked away inside the matchbox. I tip these objects into my palm – like a miniature version of my dad's biscuit tin, I am holding my mum's autobiography in my hand.

One day, my sister Kathryn asked if she could take my fossil collection to her primary school for a show and tell. We wrapped the fossils, and minerals, and crystals in dusters and packed them into two boxes, along with my geologist's hammer and my *Observer's Book of Geology*. She rehearsed her talk about her brother's rock collection, and on the day of the lesson we carried the boxes to school. I never really found out how her talk went, but, not wanting to carry the collection home she left the stones in school over the weekend. At some point during the weekend a gang of kids broke into the school and trashed the place, smashing my collection of fossils with the hammer. Thinking about it now, it's almost comical, but at the time this was heartbreaking. Kathryn's teacher sent *The Observer's Book of Geology* back home with a letter to my parents explaining what had happened. I still have it now, it's always near my desk. Whoever smashed my fossil collection also ripped the book to pieces. I taped the cover back together.

There was one surviving piece of rock – too big to take to school for the show and tell. My mother took it outside and placed it in a rockery she was building near the backyard gate. The rock was a piece of limestone, about as big as a human skull. It was covered with crustaceans, the calyx of crinoids. In time, the weather ate away at these stone-ghosts, dissolved them in rain and snow, until it was just a chunk of crumbling rock in a rough garden of campanula and dianthus. It felt like the dissolving of an obsession.

On a visit to the Museum of Natural History, my daughter Pearl, then four or five years old, became fascinated with stones. In the gift shop, she bought a small box containing twelve semi-precious fragments of rock – jasper, amber, topaz, quartz, turquoise. We sat in the café, talking about my childhood collection. I was thrilled that she was becoming a rock-hound like me, and when we were travelling home on the train to Liverpool, she suddenly let out a scream of such intensity that we thought she must be in pain. Sobbing, she told us she had left her stone collection in the museum toilets. When we got home I bought more stones on Ebay. I resented paying for them twice, but I recognised the agony of the loss.

It's the end of another Pink Floyd sunset. The dark is tarmac-black, drained of colour and light, empty. A short while ago there had been a vast display of light and dazzle. Now there is nothing.

It feels like the end of the world here, like the last days, as if people have come to witness a finality or say goodbye. I've always felt this about this beach, this estuary, this sky. People move in slow-motion. In the summer, they suddenly appear out of the heat-haze shimmer. In the winter, people in the distance move like dancers, strange choreographed shapes that could be birds but turn out to be children looking for shells, or old men with binoculars glassing the horizon. I said to Amy that it felt like the end of the world and she said she felt the same. I feel happy-sad here, filled with nostalgia and a longing for a future I fear we will never see. If this were the last day of our lives we would come here to watch the sunset and to listen to the breathing of the earth.

Underground Republic

Once I met a Radium Girl who told me stories about painting the cockpit dials in Air Force planes, how she once shone in the dark, not knowing that her luminous beauty was the cause of her mysterious diseases. I met her in a gay club called The Bear's Paw, a place where we used to go for drinks in the dead hours when the pubs were closed. I told her about my grandad and his radium implants, and in my memory, she sat there in the drinking den, glowing like a lantern in the dark; in reality, she was an old lady with an American accent and she might well have been spinning me a yarn.

I began hanging out on Mathew Street in 1974, drinking in the Grapes when it was a proper back-street pub not far from the legendary Cavern, which had been filled in and turned into a car park. In a way, this had its advantages. It meant there was no site of pilgrimage, nowhere for tourists to visit, nowhere to over-exploit and spoil. Most people couldn't even remember where the entrance to the club had been. It was just dirt and gravel and parked-up Cortinas. There was nothing to do on Mathew Street now, apart from sitting in the Grapes or the White Star and drinking Higson's beer and talking idle talk. It was bliss. I topped up my dole money with whatever cash I made selling junk on the market. I'd mooch in the bookshops and go and see bands at the Liverpool Stadium and the Mountford Hall. Hawkwind and their sonic space-rituals; The Doctors of Madness with their glam-Frankenstein singer Kid Strange; Cockney Rebel's Steve Harley walking on water, through mist; The Sensational Alex Harvey Band, and Be Bop Deluxe with guitars sounding like wild birds from outer space. I bumped into Alice Cooper at the Empire, through the loading bay as the roadies were carrying in his guillotine. I saw Lou Reed pretending to jack up on stage while he was singing *Heroin*. Doctor Feelgood's Lee Brilleaux in his filthy sky-blue suit looked like something to aspire to. When Roxy Music came to town, the glamorous crowd parading the pavements outside the Liverpool Empire looked the way I imagined Weimar-era Alexanderplatz must have looked.

I hung around with a gang of lads who were as lost as I was. We were dead-end kids with Camus in our back pockets; we got crap jobs as filing clerks and drank three pints at lunchtime. One of my jobs was to deliver post to other office blocks around the city, and I found myself wandering the streets and exploring the buildings I'd been to with my mother. In the Grapes, you'd end up drinking with Allan Williams, The Man Who Gave The Beatles Away, and Bob Wooler, the Cavern's DJ, the pair of them regaling people with Beatles anecdotes in the very pub where the Fabs once drank. It was Mersey Beat nostalgia in a city that had desecrated sacred ground by demolishing the club where it had all started.

My friends and I were waiting for something but we didn't know what it was. Sometimes we'd go down to the sea wall underneath the radar station at the mouth of the Mersey at four in the morning and watch the ships leaving on the tide. After glimpsing his portrait on the cover of *Desolation Angels* I fell in love with Jack Kerouac – even more so when I discovered he had been in Liverpool in 1943 – and I dreamed of shipping out to sea but knew I never would. So my friends and I would meet up in the Grapes, drink the days away and then we'd go home to our record players, listening for clues. Perhaps the radar station was emitting secret messages, Morse Code dots and dashes, magic spells, because things were beginning to change, the city made strange by poets and dreamers.

Peter O'Halligan had just taken over an old fruit warehouse on Mathew Street when I began to see him in the area, often sitting in the window of the Kardomah café eating his 'early riser' breakfast, rolling a fag. He looked like a beat poet or a seafarer, even more so when he began wearing what looked like an admiral's uniform. I watched with fascination as the fruit warehouse was transformed into a place called 'The Liverpool School of Language, Music, Dream and Pun', a moored ship, complete with Plimsoll Line marking the weight of the building's visionary cargo. My favourite network of streets – Mathew Street, Button Street, Rainford Square, Temple Court – now had its own strange university, like Herzog's *Fitzcarraldo* ship, a tramp steamer full of ideas and dreams, beached down a cobbled back alley, crewed by Peter and his cousin Sean Halligan (aka O'cean Halligan), photographer and poet. Essentially the building was an Arts Lab. The upstairs café, O'Halligan's Parlour, became the hangout for the city's dropouts and beatniks. On the ground floor was Aunt Twacky's Bazaar, where people came to buy clothes and records and gawp at wild characters such as bald, tutu-clad Jayne Casey; Pete Burns, who looked like a teddy boy from a distant star; and Paul Rutherford in pyjamas and leather jacket. It was a beautiful carnival, an arcade of freaks who looked like they'd walked out of a Diane Arbus photograph.

It got even better and stranger when Ken Campbell opened his Science Fiction Theatre of Liverpool in the same building. I once watched Campbell feeding lamb chops to a runty hound in the Everyman Bistro, chatting to the dog about the tenderness of the meat. He had the look of a medieval peasant in a Brueghel painting, pop-eyed like Marty Feldman and wild-haired like Ken Dodd, a commedia vagrant alive as fireworks, Max Wall cross-bred with Lear on the heath. Legend has it that when the Science Fiction Theatre of Liverpool presented its first performance of the *Illuminatus* trilogy, it was the twenty-third day of the month and twenty-three people were in the audience watching twenty-three actors battle against an organisation that secretly controls the world. Mathew Street was now an altered state and magnetic north was no longer necessary.

All of this happened just yards away from the very spot Peter O'Halligan identified as the place Carl Gustav Jung had dreamed about in 1927:

> In the centre was a round pool, and in the middle of it a small island. While everything round about was obscured by rain, fog, smoke and dimly lit darkness, the little island blazed with sunlight. On it stood a single tree, a magnolia, in a shower of reddish blossoms: the source of light. I had a vision of unearthly beauty and that was why I was able to live at all. Liverpool is the pool of life.

Night creatures emerged into the sunlight and gravitated towards O'Halligan's dream-ship. People like me, looking for something but not knowing what it was, were drawn by magnetic forces into the tiny warren of streets. Ken Campbell's set builder was the future KLF psychonaut Bill Drummond. The artist Charlie Alexander installed a huge refrigerated tank on the street with a peephole in the side, through which people said you could glimpse a preserved shark. (I looked into that peephole nearly every day and all I ever saw was darkness.) Sean Halligan and Denato Cincollo drove to Bollingen in Switzerland to collect a piece of stone from Jung's house. And into this stone the legend 'Liverpool is the pool of Life' was carved, and a bust of Jung by the artist David Wright was installed in the wall of the School in celebration of Jung's dream-visit – Jung's great grandson, Mark Balman, unveiled the plaque with the Swiss Consul General. When the Liverpool School held the Mathew Street festival in 1976, Charlie Alexander jumped into a skip full of custard. A sculpted, half-peeled banana over the entrance to Aunt Twacky's bore the legend 'O'Pun'. Halfway up the wall there was a plaque commemorating the number of times John Lennon had pissed there. Deaf School became the house band. Prunella Gee, David Rappaport, Bill Nighy and Jim Broadbent all acted at Science Fiction Theatre. The performances were anarchic, rude, chaotic, the outpourings of Ken Campbell's mind. It was a cosmic kaleidoscope in which twenty-three actors played three hundred characters, and all of this beautiful chaos spilled out into the streets, filling the labyrinth with madness.

Ley-lines ran beneath the city's pavements connecting Mathew Street to other outposts of disruption. In Probe Records on Clarence Street I bought Captain Beefheart's *Trout Mask Replica*, a record that changed the way I listened to the world. It was like stumbling across a photograph album in a jumble sale, opening it up and falling into a lunatic asylum. Liverpool is a Beefheart city, beloved of artists, poets and musicians. At an exhibition of his black-and-white paintings at the Bluecoat in April 1972, he talked about Kellogg's Corn Flakes and colour TV as the antithesis of his monochrome canvases. When I went to see him play at Rotters Club in October 1980, it was an extraordinary cacophony, like a circus pit band collaborating with the animals. Before the gig I saw him standing bemused in the street, as if he were trying to make sense of the monstrous St John's shopping precinct that housed the venue. I wanted to say hello to him but he emanated strange energies. I retreated to an outdoor escalator and rode up and down it several times, watching the magus standing there as if he were casting a spell or conducting an exorcism.

And then there was Kevin Coyne's *Marjory Razorblade*, another cabinet of curiosities. Coyne's mind was a dying seaside town: broken-windowed alehouses, charity shops, battered lives in bleak attics forgotten by everyone but him. He bawled out his songs like a dog locked out in the rain: songs of knife-tongued old ladies, Eastbourne girls flashing their knickers, Jackie in his boarding house, paper hat on his head, in the hospital on the hill where Coyne once worked. It was a desolate, desperate scrapbook of stories, a scuffed blues bestiary by England's Gogol.

The record was a downbeat companion piece to the Beefheart; it made me think of New Brighton in melancholy rain or the last ride on the dodgems before the travelling fair left town. Up a flight of stairs above Probe Records was Atticus Books, a place smelling of coffee and (so I imagined) American paperbacks; I bought Robert Anton Wilson's *Illuminatus* trilogy here, in the paperback with the yellow submarine covers. I felt connected to a subterranean encyclopaedia where names like Leary, Crowley and Kesey triggered off deeper connections, opened up maps of strange territories. Liverpool in the mid 1970s was a concatenation of postwar industrial desolation and the secret republic of the Mathew Street labyrinth. I didn't *really* believe in ley lines, but I *chose* to live in a world where ley lines could exist, and Mathew Street was on a direct line from one lodestone to another.

This was my education. I'd always wandered the streets but now I was in town most days, mapping the city, discovering new places. Instead of going to work at the Council I'd pretend I had a dental appointment and I'd go walking around Liverpool 8, drinking in Peter Kavanagh's or buying King Tubby records in Granby Street. I enjoyed getting lost. Years later, when I read Rebecca Solnit's *A Field Guide to Getting Lost*, I was quite taken by her question: 'How do you go about finding those things that are in some ways about extending the boundaries of the self into unknown territory, about becoming someone else?' I didn't know it at the time but that's what I was doing. And I didn't know how to have conversations about any of it. I didn't know what questions to ask and I didn't have anyone to put the questions to. I could recognise like-minded souls by the records they carried underneath their arm or the paperback they had tucked in their overcoat pocket, but I kept my secret society membership to one. I could send and receive signals but I didn't have the keys to the radar station.

I bought books. In News from Nowhere I bought Stewart Brand's *Whole Earth Catalogue, The Squatters Handbook*, Situationist pamphlets, samizdat publications. Atticus Books was my City Lights. Frank O'Hara's *Lunch Poems*; Ferlinghetti's *A Coney Island of the Mind*, Anna Kavan's *Ice*, Arthur Rimbaud's *Illuminations* (it was important to have the New Directions edition with the Ray Johnson cover). I read books I didn't quite understand but found incredibly exciting, like Samuel Beckett's trilogy and Céline's *Journey to the End of the Night* and *Death on the Instalment Plan*. While I was immersing myself in all this my friend Paul Simpson, of the Liverpool band The Wild Swans, was doing exactly the same – I didn't get to know Paul until I was in my fifties, even though we went to the same school. When I meet Paul now, we often talk about particular books and records – Knut Hamsun's *Hunger*, Patti Smith's *Piss Factory* – and realise we must have bought them in the same place at more or less the same time and that we'd both turned them into talismans.

In my walks around Liverpool 8 – the run-down, bohemian area I liked to imagine as Liverpool's Greenwich Village – I would often gravitate towards the art school, the one I'd always planned to go to but never did. Stuart Sutcliffe and John Lennon were students there. I would spot certain painters in the street, or drinking in Ye Cracke; people like Arthur Ballard, Sam Walsh, Maurice Cockrill. The art school was crucial to Liverpool 8's atmosphere of bohemian dissidence. Adrian Henri was everywhere; his painting *The Entry of Christ Into Liverpool* was a depiction of a mad parade of renegades: William Burroughs, Pete Brown, Charlie Mingus, George Melly, Henry Graham, Arthur Dooley, Charlie Parker, The Beatles, Alfred Jarry, Pere Ubu, processing along Lime Street past neon Guinness signs, escorting Christ into a socialist utopia. The painting is like an avant-punk street scene by L. S. Lowry, painted on exposed hessian, vibrantly alive and carnivalesque. Immersing myself in its crowd I recognised people I might well glimpse on Hope Street, or skulking down Rice Street on their way to the boozer. It was another portal into the underground.

It went on, it grew, it reverberated. The punk club Eric's opened in a Mathew Street cellar, opposite the site where the Cavern once stood. Probe Records moved down the hill to Button Street. Roger Eagle would stop you on the street and tell you to buy a Tapper Zukie record, and you would go and do as you were told and never regret it. In Eric's, on more than one occasion, I saw a dead rat in the urinal. And for less than a quid a pop, I also saw God knows how many incredible bands there, including the Ramones on the same bill as Talking Heads, Pere Ubu and the Pop Group, the Buzzcocks and the Slits. On the night I was going to see The Clash I got pulled by the police, bundled into the back of a meat wagon and driven around the city for an hour until they dumped me down the dock road in the dark, too late to see the band. Once or twice a week after the club kicked out I would walk the eight-mile journey home, past striptease pubs, dodgy car parks, dark lanes, scrapheap mountains, derelict docks and warehouses.

It never occurred to me to talk to anyone, to get involved, to participate. I was always an observer – on the margins, watching. I don't think I was ready for the radical transformation all these experiences had to offer. It felt like an immersive apprenticeship, a self-education. Sometimes, though, I'd walk home with Hoppy and when we got to his house he'd play me Henry Cow and Robert Wyatt records. *Ruth is Stranger than Richard* became another world I would live in. The band that had the most effect on me were The Fall. *What would Mark E. Smith do? What would Mark E. Smith think?* The Fall became a way of looking at the world, a lens through which to both focus and expand. Smith sang about industrial estates and psychic dancehalls, witch trials, rebellious jukeboxes and underground 'medecin', bingo-masters and city hobgoblins. I walked the city then, I walk the city now and there are certain streets – because of the winter light, because of the rain, because of the shutters and the echoing din of broken burglar alarms, and the pound-shop squalor of desolate pedestrianised streets, and the country-and-western heartbreakers on faulty jukeboxes – that summon up The Fall. As he grew older, Mark E. Smith's body and face came to resemble his gnarled and

crabby music. He became his own songs. Sometimes, I half expect to see Mark E. Smith supping a pint in a pub full of old ranters, rattling a beer mat on the table to the beat of a karaoke yelper.

I went to live in Liverpool 8, in Falkner Square, finally arriving in the place I'd always dreamed of living. In a dirt-cheap flat in a Georgian mansion I began to write poetry and plays. In the winter, when it snowed, the ceilings collapsed because thieves had stolen part of the roof. The bedroom and living room were full of dirty snow, melting into the carpets. The neighbour was a schizophrenic who let prostitutes from the Square use his place as a knocking shop. There were mattresses everywhere and a steady queue of desperate men hanging around the stairwells. The people who lived in the house backing onto ours held cockfights in the alleyway. We would watch men handing over money, betting on the birds. During the bin strike, the yard and cellar became infested with rats. When the bin men finally took the heaps of rubbish away the tarmac in the yard was a warren of rat tunnels. It was hell. So much for romance. But I lived in a place where poets had lived, where Peter Ellis my architect hero had lived, around the corner from John Lennon's house. Living the dream.

Out on the streets I walk the stations of the cross, the compass points and sacred sites of the underground republic. Somewhere, hereabouts, Robert Creeley reads his poems in Samson and Barlow's in 1964. Thelonious Monk is walking along Hope Street after performing with Art Blakey at the Philharmonic Hall on May Day, 1961. In Arthur Dooley's 1972 film *One Pair of Eyes*, the sculptor rides on a motorboat along the city's derelict Albert Dock, raging against city planners and the abandonment of the waterfront. Pulp novelist Gideon Harlax strides through a dystopian Anglican cathedral in David Rudkin's visionary TV film *Artemis 81* before climbing up into the bell tower, a concrete sarcophagus that could have been designed by H. R. Giger and filmed by Andrei Tarkovsky. I go to the pubs where Allen Ginsberg drank with Adrian Henri in May 1965 when he declared Liverpool to be 'at the present moment, the centre of consciousness of the human universe'. I walk past the building on Hardman Street where Atticus Books relocated, and where William Burroughs signed copies of his novels in 1982. I see Bob Dylan in May 1966, hanging out with street kids in the doorway of a derelict warehouse on Dublin Street. I glimpse Arthur Rimbaud, wandering through the city in 1876, on his way from Cork to Le Havre after absconding from the Dutch army. By the time Ken Kesey's Merry Pranksters turned up in Mathew Street in 1999 it was too late. The Liverpool School was long gone and Peter O'Halligan had gone deeper into his own search for secret knowledge. Mathew Street was over, theme-parked, desolate of meaning.

But then, one day I go back there, drawn back by the man who started it all. I stand with Pearl and Amy on a manhole cover at an unveiling of a commemorative plaque, listening to Peter O'Halligan talking about the Liverpool School of Language, Music, Dream and Pun. It's December 2012 and Peter is explaining how this building on this street stands on a meridian. The street is now a hell hole of tourist bars and stag-and-hen parties, abysmal statues of Cilla Black and John Lennon, brawling drunks and permanent two-for-one happy hours. Jung leans out of his hole-in-the-wall of a pub that used to be a ship of dreams. Saddened, we stand in a place of memories in the labyrinth of my youth.

Black Streams

Gazing up at Martin's Bank on Water Street, I see an octopus carved into the underside of a stone balcony – a mythical beast swimming in stone above the heads of oblivious pedestrians. There are dolphins and lobsters, starfish and seahorses sculpted and carved into bank doorways and office-block facades. The city is an aquarium of stone sea creatures; there are mermen above us, waiting for the waters to rise.

On the front wall of the old Yates's Wine Lodge building in Moorfields, where years ago we used to drink Aussie White on our way to see The Fall or some other band of renegades at Eric's club, the artist Richard Wilson cut an ovoid disc, eight metres in diameter, on a giant mechanical pivot. This artwork, *Turning the Place Over,* all 26 tonnes of spinning wall and window, resembles a record in an enormous jukebox. To stand in the street and watch part of this building rotate in three dimensions above your head was a breathtaking spectacle, a perforation in the city's fabric like something you might glimpse in Christopher Nolan's *Inception.* Even now, years after the wall has stopped turning, you can still see the circular incision in the facade, as if someone has cut into it with a gigantic hole saw. Wilson's automaton turned a condemned, derelict eyesore into a thing of beauty, an 'active void' that brought attention to the abandoned and the overlooked.

Today, the building is surrounded by car parks and the dead-eyed facade of Moorfields station. For a few short years this was a street graced by imagination, wit and invention, a mechanical theatre of wonder, cocking a snook at the usual Council quango dreck bereft of even a spark of ingenuity. Less than half a mile from here the mayor's cloud-scrapers are stacking up like filing cabinets along the waterfront, a celebration of the monstrous, the cynical and the pointless. Five billion quid's worth of vacuity, 315,000 square metres of conference and leisure facilities which no one with any sense or imagination will ever want to use. It occurs to me one night as I stand before these structures that represent the banality of consumption that they resemble inverted barcodes.

In the days when my mother was dying I walked restlessly around the city day after day, mad with the conviction that I could stop her dying by walking and remembering the streets we explored when I was a child and she was young and death was distant, impossible. I remember the day I asked my mother if everybody died, and she replied, 'You won't die. You're going to live forever...' I think she said this out of kindness, because she didn't want to frighten me, but the consequence of those simple words meant I spent the rest of my life morbidly obsessed with death: not just with *my* death or the death of those near me, but with the death of animals and forests and stars, – and buildings. I walked the city when she was dying, looking for the empty spaces where old buildings had disappeared. I walked the streets she taught me to love. I stood in front of buildings and in car parks trying to remember what used to be there. A building had been erased – that word again – and my memory of the building had also been erased. The city suffered from some kind of built-in amnesia, as if it didn't want to remember or even think about its own wounds. It seemed to stoically accommodate absence and loss.

How do you make a city better? No one seems to know. But they *do* know how to make a city worse. Where some might

see *Turning the Place Over* as visionary art, others see a tourist attraction. Perhaps there was a chance, when Liverpool was European Capital of Culture in 2008, to rediscover a city of visions and dreams. But by then the City Council had already flogged forty-two acres of Liverpool to a Duke who built a massive shopping centre.

I suppose it's always been this way, and always will be.

A short walk from Wilson's masterpiece there are two visionary buildings designed by Peter Ellis. Yet they were hardly appreciated in their time. In 1866, *The Builder* magazine wrote of the Oriel Chambers: 'Did we not see this vast abortion – which would be depressing were it not ludicrous – with our own eyes, we should have doubted the possibility of its existence. Where and in what are their beauties supposed to lie?' It's December, dark at 4 o'clock, nakedly cold; the pubs are rammed with Christmas drunks and I'm wandering the streets. I stand outside the Oriel Chambers. To call it an office building diminishes it, because this building is a dream. *Where and in what are their beauties supposed to lie?* Women wait for taxis, shivering in the cold night air. Men smoke in doorways, gawping at the women in their skimpy party dresses. And I'm watching the building, trying to understand its strange beauty.

Have you ever seen the Oriel Chambers? I sometimes think it belongs in a steampunk version of Lisbon. When I read the great Portuguese poet Fernando Pessoa's unfinished masterpiece *The Book of Disquiet,* I imagine him – or rather his heteronym Bernardo Soares – writing his deepest thoughts into a ledger inside this building. Whenever I visit Lisbon I expect its buildings to look like the Oriel Chambers, but only the Elevador de Santa Justa seems to belong in this fantasy. Oriel Chambers was once described as '*a cellular habitation for the human insect*', which makes it sound like a futuristic structure in a city designed by China Miéville.

In an alternative history of Liverpool, Ellis would have carried on building his dreams but, perhaps because his ideas were so badly received, the work dried up. An amateur historian once told me Peter Ellis *invented* Chicago. When the American architect John Wellborn Root visited Liverpool in the late 1860s he looked closely at Ellis's two buildings. Back in America he built the Rookery Building, inspired by his study of the Oriel Chambers and Ellis's other masterpiece at 16 Cook Street, which resembles an elegant warehouse or a vast, vertical glass-and-stone doorway. And through that doorway, rising from floor to rooftop, there is a spiral staircase of such breathtaking audacity that sometimes I climb the stairs just for the joy of it. It's like climbing into a cabinet of wonders, or discovering a secret world inside a gigantic grandfather clock.

I keep walking through the night to the Pier Head, where I like to come and visit a ventilation shaft for the Mersey Tunnel. It's described as a vent shaft but it's actually an Art Deco spaceship pointing towards the heavens, piloted by Mercury, the messenger of the Gods. On board this Portland Stone rocket designed by Herbert J. Rowse in 1934 there is Mercury, seemingly wearing a pair of pilot's flying goggles, and there are two black basalt figures called Day and Night, one transporting the sun into space, the other delivering a star. Sometimes I visit them just to touch their smooth black skin. Beneath my feet there are secret engines, iron lungs, filling the road under the Mersey with oxygen. When I was a child we used to touch Night and Day for luck whilst gazing up at Mercury as he prepared to blast into space. Rowse the architect, and Edmund Thompson and George Capstick, the sculptors who designed these stone astronauts, smuggled some kind of Ancient Egyptian Futurism into the city and passed it off as an air vent.

At the same time that Thompson and Capstick were creating the basalt gods of Day and Night, Henry Tyson Smith was carving sea creatures into many of the city's buildings: mermen and starfish, dolphins and seahorses. He also sculpted the cenotaph in Lime Street, commemorating the men from Liverpool who died in the First World War.

These people – Smith, Ellis, Rowse, Thompson, Capstick – had beautiful ideas and for a short time they were allowed to weave their visions onto the fabric of the city. Near the tunnel entrance, Thomas Shelmerdine's Imperial Chambers is Liverpool's Flatiron Building, a terracotta slice with a domed roof that looks like it belongs on a sharp corner in Gotham. You can touch this building and feel the ideas within its materials. It is sensual and tactile, visually thrilling, as if Shelmerdine wanted to give the people of Liverpool *pleasure* as they went about their day. But here's the thing – the building has been ruined. On top of the Imperial roof there's an ugly black storage box. For some inexplicable reason this insult was granted 'retrospective planning permission' by the Council. The Imperial is now the football-themed Shankly Hotel and its owner is a close friend of the Mayor.

Lately, I've decided to become a geomancer. I'm convinced that the city is suffering from geopathic stress, from the negative energy of 'black streams'. The city is depressed because its immune system is broken, and while it is slumbering in a kind of chronic fatigue syndrome that afflicts neglected cities, the warlocks and hobgoblins move in and ransack the place, which leads to blindness, paranormal activity and a surplus of wedding hotels.

I've decided to exorcise the city's demons through the act of walking. I walk from one architectural disaster to another: from Commutation Row to the Shankly Hotel, from there to the Hilton, then the Mann Island Development on the waterfront. I stride contemptuously past St John's Precinct and the Clayton Square shopping centre. I walk down Lime Street, casting ritual spells as I go, mourning the vanished cinemas and remembering Stanley Reynold's article 'The Museum of the Horrifying Example' – he wasn't talking about black streams of negative property development, but he might as well have been.

One summer's day I'm walking with Amy and Pearl, showing

them some of my favourite places – places I've been visiting since I was a child. We stop at a café for a pot of tea. It's a beautiful day so we sit outside, enjoying the rare summer sun. As we sit, watching the world, I remember to look up – 'Always look up!' as my mother used to say. And there, on the underside of a Portland Stone balcony is the carving I first saw long ago when I was young. I later discover that the sculpture I'm admiring was by Tyson Smith. It's an octopus, its tentacles spread like the rays of a strange sun. To me it is a symbol of light and optimism – a spell to banish the darkness of black streams.

The Furys

I go walking down Stanley Road in Kirkdale where my dad used to have two junk shops selling house-clearance wardrobes, dressing tables, clutter. Ships from Southeast Asia would dock on the Mersey and Malaysian seamen would come and barter for Singer sewing machines. They'd walk back down the hill, a single-file crocodile of sailors with treadle sewing machines balanced on their heads. Old women would come in and talk about their superstitions. They would leave the shop if there was a bird ornament or painting. Once a woman crossed herself because we were selling a picture of a sparrow.

In the 1970s and 1980s, after the demolitions, there were vast empty wastes here, what we called The Debris or The Hollow – the 'oller'. At weekends illegal flea markets sprang up, hunting grounds for bargain scroungers and collectors and a place to top up the dole. We sold books, pots and pans, half-full cans of paint, hub caps, dolls houses, busted radios, records, accordions, cutlery, anything to make a quid. I once saw five fairground dodgem cars for sale, ten quid a piece. Scavengers from Bidston tip across the river would dump their gleanings on the dirt. Old men came with prams full of suitcases and the cases were full of treasure.

Strange men walked here. The Dog King had ropes tied around his body, and at the end of each rope was a dog, a hound from Hell. He was then dragged, staggering in whichever direction the strongest or hungriest dog wanted to go – the man was demonic, wild-haired and bloodshot-eyed, striding in ripped wellingtons and army raincoat, howling and spitting, as if he were a dog himself. He was a terrifying vision of flailing limbs, mongrel hunger and violence. The debris wastelands of the city were his territories. He once came up so close to me I could see into his skull. In the upstairs room of a derelict shop on Stanley Road I once found a heap of burnt bones in a fireplace. I imagined this was the Dog King's lair – where he cooked his mongrels.

Another old man who haunted the market was Eric, who collected 78s. His holdalls were full of brittle shellac discs – music-hall tunes, palm-court orchestras, end-of-the-pier novelty vocalists, monologists, all songs no one else wanted. The ground was always unsteady beneath Eric's feet and he liked to blame it on 'the undulating terrain'. I suspect he was always drunk. He was fat as a barrage balloon and his skull was bald as a boulder. We used to flog him records on Westminster Road market, twenty pence a disc. He would finger the grooves gently, as if he were caressing a silk stocking. 'Now, let's see if we can come to some sort of arrangement', the word stretched – *arraaaaanngement.* Like W. C. Fields playing a carnie huckster, he'd finger in his purse for some copper coins, a pittance to pay for gold dust. The erotics of collecting.

We used to sell ornaments to Orlando Paso the boxer, undefeated Welterweight Champion of Nigeria, winner of the 1958 Collister Belt, a lover of gaudy trinkets, his pockets always full of signed photographs. He'd come to Liverpool in the 1960s to fight at the boxing stadium and for some reason he had never left. Now he was a gentle soul rummaging through boxes full of trinkets, buying Crying Boy paintings when nobody else wanted them because it was a cursed image that caused houses to burn down. All over the market there were paintings of crying boys and the only person buying them was a boxer from Nigeria.

Everything was provisional, temporary. It was as if the world's flotsam had gathered itself here on the wastelands of Liverpool, and people had come, drawn by secret signals and an underground language, by hunger and economic necessity to root and scavenge and meet and talk. Because the markets weren't licensed they had a defiant, subversive, anti-authority atmosphere. The people gathered here might have been descendants of Winstanley's Diggers, occupying the land. Sometimes the police would come and try to move people on, or someone from the Council would come with a clipboard and reluctantly take people's names, not really believing in the task, knowing that everyone was giving false names and addresses anyway. Sometimes there were fights, territorial bickering over prime pitches, thieving. The city was going through the process of 'managed decline' inflicted on it by Thatcher and Howe. If there were no jobs and you were signing on then 'working on the side' was the obvious, pragmatic choice. Every few months bulldozers would come and block the debris off with mounds of rubble and the word would go around that the market had moved on to another hollow, and the vans and prams and barrows would scatter and descend on the new site.

I bought rare blues records here – Howlin' Wolf, Sleepy John Estes, Blind Lemon Jefferson; ex-jukebox reggae 45s by people like Alton Ellis and Derrick Morgan. In a box of Top of the Pops and James Last LPs, I found Charlie Mingus's *Ah Um*, its Fujita sleeve damaged by rain. In my bedroom, I dropped the needle on 'Goodbye Pork Pie Hat' over and over again. An elegy for Lester Young, it aches with pain and loss. It felt like the right music for the shadows of my room. It felt the way I wanted to feel – nocturnal, lonely, sombre – and it felt, still feels, like the soundtrack to this wounded city. When I walk down the beat-up streets of Kirkdale, Mingus is in my thoughts.

In the debris, there were books looted from abandoned libraries; strange dictionaries, maps. A dealer called Gerard Reid would rummage through the boxes of ten-pence books I was selling, pull one out of the pile and say, 'Read it, don't sell it.' Through

Gerard I discovered Irish writers – Yeats, Brendan Behan, the Blasket Island chroniclers. Once, I found a heap of dime-store sci fi: Philip K. Dick, Harlan Ellison, Theodore Sturgeon; a stash of Beat Generation rare editions; a City Lights *Lunch Poems* by Frank O'Hara, and a Calder & Boyars edition of Beckett's translation of Apollinaire's 'Zone'; 'You are alone morning is at hand/In the streets the milk men rattle their cans/Like a dark beauty night withdraws'. It was just like the mornings in the market: 6am, night pulling away from the city and the weather seeming to change when the day lit up the rabble; rummaging through piles of dead men's clothes, prayer books, light falling on an apostle spoon, turning it into silver. I found another Beckett book, *Stories and Texts for Nothing*. I sat in the back of the van out of the rain reading 'The Expelled'.

> Memories are killing. So you must not think of certain things, of those that are dear to you, or rather you must think of them, for if you don't there is the danger of finding them, in your mind, little by little. That is to say, you must think of them for a while, a good while, every day several times a day, until they sink forever in the mud.

Another man I bought books off was a blow-in from out of town. I asked him why he was selling his books and he told me he'd just split up with his wife, had nowhere to live and didn't want to be reminded of her by the books that used to share the shelves with hers. He came back the following week and this time he had his dog with him, a beautiful red setter. At the end of the day I saw the dog running wildly up and down the main road, whimpering, frightened, barking at passing cars. I tried to catch him but he escaped, running madly across the street. I went looking for the man but he had packed up and gone, never to be seen again. He'd abandoned his dog because he had been abandoned and there was nothing else to do. The cruelty of despair. When the market packed up, lost souls fought over all the crap the sellers had left behind. The people had been left behind, too. They were stray dogs, all of them were lost.

There was terrible hardship here. The saddest month was December, in the bleak midwinter grind towards Christmas, when you'd see people buying threadbare clothes, broken toys and board games with missing pieces. I once saw a woman retrieve a Barbie Doll from a skip. She cleaned it with Lucozade, wiped it down with a snot-rag, held it up to the light and nodded, satisfied that it was good enough to give as a gift.

Markets are meeting places: hives of rumour, speculation, gossip, arguments. In one of their regular acts of stupidity Liverpool City Council demolished, in the 1960s, the glorious Victorian market, a place you might have found in Barcelona or Athens. They replaced it with the banal St John's Precinct, the largest shopping centre in the city, and Liverpool has never had a decent market since.

Walking along Stanley Road, I see an old man kneeling on the ground, praying to a paving stone. The image of him resonates like a frequency. His muttering incantations overlay a memory of the younger me selling Bibles for fifty pence on The Hollow, and then bind to the vision of a woman called May, who worked in the tobacco factory and had gin-induced palsy, and would cross herself with her rosary beads every time she saw a bird.

If I had passed this corner ten minutes later I might not have seen the kneeling man, but because I have seen him he takes his place in my collection of images. My perception of this street is altered, informed by this image that enters my consciousness. And my perception of this city and my life lived within it is formed out of this mad kaleidoscope of images, like a slide-show carousel of dreams. Walking enhances – advances – this process, this assembling of mental clutter to sift and sort, to order and dismantle and rebuild. To look at it another way, perhaps my mind is the market stall or the junk shop, full of broken Gabbanelli accordions and shoeboxes full of rosary beads and apostle spoons.

James Hanley is walking down Lambeth Road, looking for his

characters. His novel *The Furys* takes place in and around these streets. The book was one of my market treasures, a Chatto & Windus first edition with a cover showing a montage of steam ships, slums, cloth-capped men and a waif wrapped in a shawl. Discovering that Hanley had lived in one of these streets and that he set the novel in the area was thrilling. The story seems to take place in the 1930s, although the epic street battle at the heart of the drama is clearly an enactment of the general transport strike rally in August 1911, when, on Bloody Sunday, a police battalion charged the crowd of 85,000 people – 350 people were injured, 3,500 troops were stationed in the city and the 18th Hussars opened fire on a crowd on Vauxhall Road, killing two men and injuring over a dozen others. Set against this backdrop, the book is a closely observed portrait of a family disintegrating under the pressures of working-class struggle, strikes and mob violence in the parlours, kitchens, streets, engine yards and docks. It's like a Scouse Dostoyevsky novel and you can smell the decay.

Hanley observes the family so closely it's as if he is living in their house, like a lodger who tiptoes to his attic cot and writes down the family's every move. I place the book alongside *Distant Voices, Still Lives* in my personal museum of Liverpool life. James Hanley pulled the story from these streets, painted the Fury family from characters he must have seen in the terraces lining the hill. Those characters are still here. An old man is looking over the canal bridge at a floating dismembered doll. His boxer's face is a mess, a face that looks like it was ripped to pieces and glued back together by someone who lost interest. I look away up the hill, and when I look back the man has disappeared.

The Lighthouse pub is boarded up, but there's a boy sitting on the step eating crisps, just the way boys used to when the pub was up and running and the dads were inside sipping their pints of brown and mild. Perhaps the men are still inside behind the shutters in the eternal lock-in of their dreams. I can see Mr Fury from Hanley's book:

Mr Fury's head hung perilously near his glass. He had fallen asleep. The bar-room was empty. A big fire burnt in the grate. The barman looked across at the sleeping man and smiled. The door opened. A tall, heavily built man came in and stood at the counter. He called for a drink. He turned around and looked at the man whose head was gradually drooping lower and lower. The man went across and drew the glass away … The dozing man sat up with fright. He had been dreaming. As he opened his eyes he imagined the bar-room to be full of people, and that all these people were staring at him. The newcomer sat down beside him. Mr Fury stared stupidly at the froth now settling in his glass. He turned his head sharply and a flash of spit struck the open gate.

I cannot accurately map the book onto these streets and so I improvise, deciding this is Mr Fury's local and he is in there now, on the nod over his pint of Falstaff. Once, sitting drinking in the Lighthouse, I looked out into the street and saw the Duke of Edinburgh sitting in a limousine, waiting for the traffic lights to change.

The old Grosvenor cinema, one of the many Liverpool picture houses designed by my mum's boss Alfred Shennan, is now a funeral parlour, which seems somehow apt and touching; a three-act drama in architectural form, from childhood Saturday matinee to middle-aged bingo parlour to coffin house. I have a vivid memory of coming here to watch *Daleks – Invasion Earth* in 1966, but this is impossible because the Grosvenor closed as a cinema in 1963. When it was a bingo parlour women used to come into the junk shop and spend their winnings. I remember a woman who always seemed to be crying. I once asked her name and she replied, 'Just call me Blocked Tear Ducts. Everybody else does.'

Kirkdale slouches down the hill towards the old tobacco factory on the canal, beyond that the docks, beyond that the empty river. Streets of neat terraces called Crocus, Harebell, Daisy, Pansy, Snowdrop and Woodbine, 'facing the sea like so many dogs, barking out their defiance of time and change,' as Hanley puts it. As recently as the 1960s at Daisy Street school, Protestant and

Catholic children were kept apart at play time and had different dinner times and going-home times. The old wastelands where the markets were held are now a network of suburban houses. As I walk by St John's church with its Pugin & Pugin altar, everything seems eerily quiet. I change the mood of the street by layering Mingus over the emptiness, providing it with a theme tune to an imaginary film. The funeral parlour will become the cinema it used to be and the dead will come to the screening.

Lamp posts are covered in stickers for escort agencies, guerrilla protests, 'Adios Senor Pussycat', Sharpie scrawls, 'Fuck Trump'. 'Free Mo' is spray-painted on walls and shutters, over and over again, a demand for the release of a local dealer, inside on firearms charges. On another wall in lurid red paint, 'PEEDO'. Shuttered shops, shuttered pubs, but at least the betting shop is open. A tiny man stands in the doorway twisting his betting slips into the shape of a cigarette, as if he's about to smoke his own bad luck.

I stop at the spot where one of our shops once stood. I remember Mick the window cleaner always had what he called a 'nuddie magazine' rolled up inside his jacket. He'd let you have a peep, opening up his jacket as if he were opening the curtains in a burlesque club. Inside his jacket there would be a half-naked girl showing you her breasts or knickers, 'a bit of skirt without the skirt', as Mick used to say. I sometimes went to Mick's for a cup of tea in his terraced house on Fountains Road. He used to salvage scaffolding planks and floorboards from collapsing buildings for firewood. He wouldn't chop the boards up, he'd just stick one end of the scaff plank into the flames, pushing the burnt end into the fire with his boot, the rest of the plank sticking out into his parlour. The plank would burn, slowly getting shorter, and when there was no plank left Mick would go out, break into dead tenements with a hammer and crowbar and pull up another floorboard. There was always stuff to steal in the 'derries'. Mick would load Belfast sinks, larders and mangles onto his home-made barrow and wheel it all up to the market, ciggy stump wedged between his brown and yellow teeth.

The streets match my mood. The streets *are* my mood. There's a low-level depression, a shadow of defeat. The place feels crestfallen, disappointed in its circumstances. I'm walking these streets with a restless anxiety, a vague feeling that I need to find some memories I've misplaced. If I can retrieve those memories and restore them to their rightful place, inside myself, assembled with all the other memories, maybe I will be less jagged, less fragmented. They might be in these paving stones, or shuttered up behind that closed-down pub or shop. The neighbourhood is lost and no one is helping it find itself, or find whatever it needs to make itself better. This patch of the city is a lost soul, troubled, insomniac. Violence has been done to it. This is probably an absurd thing to say, but this place is myself.

I keep walking. I walk up and down the terraced streets and across new empty spaces. Houses were built on the old market sites; these were in turn demolished and the people who lived in them were moved on. On new empty places, new houses were built. It's an endless churning process of build, demolish, build, and at every stage people are decanted, and the place loses its community and character. Perhaps it's a deliberate eradication of community, a process of unsettlement.

I lose my way. I feel slightly nervous. I'm wearing the wrong clothes. I don't know these streets as well as I used to. Stories of gangsters, drugs money and guns reel through my thoughts and unsettle me. But I can't stop walking, enacting the ritual. I believe in walking as an act of transformative magic. By walking through the place with a particular set of intentions and attitudes, maybe I can change it.

I imagine a long-forgotten songline running beneath the tarmac of these streets, a dream track. If you could unearth the lines then maybe petrosomatoglyphs would reveal themselves; symbols embedded and etched in paving stone and brick, the footprints of ancestors and animals, signs to be decoded, unleashing the mythic and folkloric potential of this place. The buried and forgotten songs, stories, dances of the place would come up to the surface. Maybe the boarded-up pubs would unclose themselves and if you went inside, the saloon would be full of pub singers – men like the great dock-road singer Kenny Docherty, 'Man of a Thousand Songs', who sang like Nat King Cole on Sunday afternoons in sawdust-floored boozers. Memory is the shadow, and behind the shadow of the boarded-up pub is the shadow of my past.

I haven't found James Hanley. I haven't even found the house he lived in. The Furys, though, are everywhere. Broken men and women – or men and women who would be broken if they didn't have the steel of dignity in their hearts. In an upstairs window, a woman's naked back: Man Ray's *Ingres' Violin* come to life in Kirkdale. I remember the too-tall man in the gabardine mac and beret who stood on Spellow Lane, every day, all day for no apparent reason. When I think of Fanny in Hanley's novel *Fanny Fury*, I remember Madge Jeffers of Newman Street, battered by grief and illness, but dignified and determined, an optimist in a terraced house, with buckets catching the rain as it poured through the roof. That Terence Davies image of rainfall inside the house isn't just a poetic vision, it's reality.

These memories spin me back into my own life and I remember my dad coming home in the rain and producing from beneath his yellow cycling cape a stray dog he's brought home. Me, throwing cushions at it, frightened of it for weeks, until it becomes my best friend and we name him after Dixie Dean. I remember the great Everton player Alex Young – the Golden Vision – ruffling my hair in Auntie Dot's corner shop on my first day at school, wishing me luck. Alex Young! I remember my mum putting clothes through the mangle, listening to *Two-Way Family Favourites*, singing along to 'A White Sport Coat' and 'A Pink Carnation'. I remember the nightmare of Tate & Lyle's factory, that monstrous coal-black beast, blasting out steam and smoke.

I have a final memory of the junk shop. I walk up the rickety stairs to the top floor and it is full of pigeons. Thieves have stolen the slates off the roof, the rain is dripping into wet cardboard boxes full of broken-backed Bibles, apostle spoons, encyclopaedias, bed-warmers, fire-irons, gutted mantle clocks. There is pigeon shit everywhere, and in the fireplace there are two tiny squabs, beaks open. It's like a props store for a stage production of Hanley's book, but in the midst of it there's the horror of those doomed birds. All these years later I stand on the pavement where the shop used to be, remembering walking away from those trapped birds.

On Everton Valley where the Lyric Theatre once stood I finally get a glimpse of James Hanley as he stands in the shadows observing the man and woman he has written into existence. Here come Mr and Mrs Fury, Mr Fury alighting from the tram and joining the queue for the theatre. Mr Fury's eyes are fastened on the street entertainer performing 'an amazing series of acrobatic feats in the street … this gentleman's completely bald head looked like a giant ivory ball. As he tossed and tumbled, he beat a most ecstatic accompaniment upon two large table-spoons … They could see the man was old, and that he hadn't a tooth in his head … ' Inside the theatre – where Mr Fury refuses to stand for the National Anthem – the air smells of tobacco and newly peeled oranges. I stand at the back of this ghost-theatre, watching the comedian, watching Mr Fury laughing, watching them go to the bar for a wet, a lemon dash and a Bass. These people could be my grandparents having a rare night out on the town. I stand in Everton Valley where the Lyric used to be and suddenly there is nothing, just a scattering of birds whooshing the memories away. I turn for home.

The Haunted Lullaby

Whate I was a child I used to lie awake at night, listening to a
woman whispering and singing men's names. The woman
floated outside my bedroom window, draped in veils and a tattered
gown, and she held her crooked fingers out, beckoning men to
come to her and kiss her. In my imagination, she was tethered to
the window ledge by ropes of golden hair. She was breathtakingly
beautiful and terrifying and it was only the closed curtains that
kept me safe – if the curtains had been open she'd have hooked me
in her claws and dragged me into the night, across the rooftops of
Liverpool to some kind of ecstatic doom. I never looked beyond
the curtains, I simply imagined her, anchored there, singing her
strange lullaby. I was scared of her but also somehow in love with
her and fifty years later I still think of her, look for her and write
about her over and over again.

I don't know if I realised it then but I was living in a story.
Every night I would rewrite and elaborate on the basic plot; my
imagination added details, made it scarier, made it more fantastic
– and yet more real, until, eventually I was living in a gothic
nightmare. The more detail I added – a twitching curtain, a
beckoning finger, an even more terrifying version of her with two
heads – the longer I stayed awake.

When I recall my childhood now, I think of disturbed sleep,
medical potions, illustrated books of fairy tales, and a kind of

phantasmagorical lantern show that my mind projected onto the walls of my room. Curtains and linoleum alive with nightmare cartoons projected from my skull.

The old house was next door to The Winslow Pub and opposite Everton football ground. The pub fascinated me; it was a dangerous place, men smoked cigarettes there, spat in the doorway, made illegal bets on horses and dogs, smelled of boozy yeast. A young woman called Elsie worked behind the bar; she had a tatty beehive hairdo and wore tight skirts like Elsie Tanner in *Coronation Street*, and lashings of mascara. I think she lived above the pub, and sometimes I would see her in the corner shop, buying fags from Auntie Dot. In the memory I have invented for her, she survives on salt-and-vinegar crisps. Her dad is the rag-and-bone man.

One bonfire night I stayed out late and when I was coming home I could hear the voice of the dead woman drifting from the alley that separated our house from the pub. I went to bed scared. The voice echoed; it called a man's name. I plucked up the courage to look through the curtains down at the back alley and there I saw Elsie the barmaid having sex with a drunk from the pub. I realised then that what I had been listening to, night after night, was the voice of Elsie calling customers down the alley for a quick one up against the backyard wall. I watched the drunkard touching Elsie's thighs and heard her whisper his name.

'Harold... Harry...'

This was magical, erotic fuel for my imagination. Hardly a day goes by when I don't remember those nights. In some ways, I think this is what made me a writer; it's the origin story for the way I see and hear Liverpool. Elsie's lullaby seeps into the city, haunting it, disturbing it, creating endless, restless turmoil. It's beautiful and strange.

I walk the city with my daughter just as my mother used to walk with me. I place her on the medieval Sanctuary Stone on Castle Street and I tell her to say anything she wants to say and nobody can stop her. There's a robin standing near her feet, singing to the streetlights. My daughter says, 'Grandma is here. She's that Robin Redbreast.' And we stand there on the Sanctuary Stone with my mother in the guise of a robin flitting about our feet.

Suddenly in the November night the city resembles a half-erased chalkboard. My daughter's drawings of big-eyed buildings and magical birds flying to broken-plate moons are layered over earlier images: of graving docks, puppet shows, graffiti saying 'Scrap Polaris' and 'No Popery', men sitting by the window in the long-vanished Kardomah Café.

You can hear it too: ship's horns, hooves of heavy horses, the street cries of hawkers, punk-rock jukeboxes, tram wires, shipbuilder's hammers, karaoke caterwauling, hymns from the floating Mariners' Church, Mersey Beat guitars. You can hear it mangled in the river weather. A haunted sound archive unleashed.

I am teaching my daughter the city, but we have to look harder for the alchemy because – according to the regeneration brochure – this is now a city of investment, digital and technology sectors, the UK's leading leisure and business destination, full of opportunities driving future prosperity. The magic is leaching out of the city, the shadows and alleyways are emptying, and so we walk through wastelands where the magic used to be, we gather autumn leaves from gutters and dirt from the rubble of demolished sacred places, and we make collages that act as pagan spells against dead imaginations.

I tell her the story of Elsie Barmaid. I show her where my grandfather used to drive his horses and their carts loaded with ice, tobacco, oats and tea in the days when the city smelled of horse manure and echoed to the sound of iron-rimmed wheels on cobbles. I show her where he used to live and where he walked, tapping his blind man's stick.

And in a play called *Family Values* written for the Unity Theatre in 1992, I took my grandfather's identification with the city one step further; he loved the city so much that he actually became it, in bed in his attic room he transformed into bricks and mortar and the lost buildings of Liverpool burst forth through his skin.

For a while in the 1990s, I lived in Cornwall, and when I moved back to Liverpool I tried to bring the Cornwall wildness with me into the city. It meant I could see the peregrines and hear the foxes barking in the night. I could see seals rolling over in the Mersey, close to where children played on the promenade, see green parakeets flying past Tesco and buzzards circling the multistorey car park. The wildness changed the city, made a menagerie of it. I decided I could transform the city through imaginative acts.

I'm walking the city, dowsing for gallows, workhouses, orphanages, plague pits, famine graves, making biro patterns in my *A to Z*, mapping occult sites and disquiet, a thirteenth month between November and December, the night like charcoal smog, the place my face was stung by hailstones.

And the city has other guardian spirits wandering through the kaleidoscope of muses. Jack Kerouac is forever drunk and wild-eyed here, playing billiards in the seamen's mission, and Gerard Manley Hopkins is seeing constellations of stars on the pavements where he used to write his sermons. Herman Melville is still walking through the immense fortresses of the docks. And Arthur Rimbaud – who haunted these streets in 1876 – is drinking rum in the ghost-saloons of long demolished pubs on Commutation Row. They seep into the city, these poets and dreamers: De Quincey the opium eater, Ginsberg and Burroughs, Bob Dylan, Malcolm Lowry, Ken Campbell, Ken Kesey, Captain Beefheart, Sun Ra, Cavafy, Patti Smith and Carl Gustav Jung, subverting and undermining the developer's dross. They are in the sediment and condensation, seeping through portal cracks in paving stones, a science-fiction collapsing of temporal zones, bleeding into the back-alley shadows of Liverpool.

Elsie the barmaid, my floating woman, will never know I still think of her or that I've written about her many times over the years. She's in my play *Rag and Bone*, where she haunts a ruined garden. She's in *Bright Phoenix*, where she represents the drunken, rebel soul of the city and sings 'Put the Blame On Mame' like Rita Hayworth in the dust of demolition.

One evening, while waiting for the last bus home, I find myself helping an old woman up off the pavement. She is drunk, weeping inconsolably. She wets herself, she screams and swears and slaps me in the face. I ask someone to help me, to phone for an ambulance, but no one helps. Eventually the man from the kebab shop makes a phone call and when the paramedics come they wearily tell me that they pick this woman up most nights of the week. But they'll take her to the hospital and check that she's okay. And as they lead her to the ambulance one of them says, 'Come on Elsie ...' Maybe this is Elsie Barmaid.

In the Walker Art Gallery, where I used to play as a child, I stand in front of a painting called *The Punishment of Lust* by Giovanni Segantini. In this remarkable, haunting painting the spirits of women, draped in veils and tattered gowns, float in a strange world, anchored by their hair, seemingly damned to a purgatorial suspension above the permafrost of what looks like a nuclear winter. It's the source of one of the abiding images from my childhood; it's the place where Elsie dwells when she isn't floating outside my childhood bedroom window, in my haunted lullaby. She's there in the desolate wastes, tethered by the ropes of her hair. I want to set her free. What if I cast a spell and release the women in Segantini's painting and let them loose in the city? What if you could change the city by imagining it differently to the way the PR companies sell it? What if the women go and haunt the hideous apartment blocks and empty offices of the bogus Futuropolis being built by property developers masquerading as politicians? What if they're hanging, anchored from the window ledges of the Mayor's bedroom? Who is to tell me I can't do that? Who is to tell me I haven't already done so ...

This is what I'm writing now. I'm writing magic spells to ward off death, to set the Muses free.

Bright Phoenix

It began with a fox.

I was sitting outside my house one warm summer evening, shortly after dusk, with my friend Paul Simpson. Our house is close to the river, beneath an enormous sky, and when night falls, if the street lights are broken, our street is plunged into charcoal darkness. As a car drove slowly down the street we saw the feral embers of a fox's eyes. It moved in slow motion, mouth full of takeaway wrapper, aware it was being watched. Then it dissolved into shadow, back into the dark.

It occurred to me that this fox would make a powerful familiar, an animal guide that I could adopt as a spirit of place. I'd been thinking about a fugitive version of the city that coexists with the real one, an occult echo, rather like the mirror cities of Besźel and Ul Qoma in China Miéville's *The City and the City*. This is where the inconvenient and awkward live. This is the city I prefer. I like people who don't belong and don't want to. I like the places where those people congregate: the back alleys and boozers, the doorways around the corner, the invisible city where ghosts dwell. I took the fox to be an emblem of this shadow-city. The word 'feral' is often used as an insult; I wanted to reclaim it by putting the animal back. The people I loved were feral creatures, disobedient and wild and kin to beast. I saw the same quality in the buildings and streets I loved – there were feral buildings and streets, damaged and wayward, neglected, overlooked and dispossessed.

And I often thought about people from childhood and school, the ones who didn't belong, who slipped through the cracks, who went unnoticed – the boy who smelled of wet-the-bed; the fat boy who looked like he belonged in the 1930s; the boy who smelled of phlegm; the boy with terrible skin and an asthma contraption. Half-forgotten stories began to emerge from the depths of memory: the boy who was blinded with a fishing hook; the kid who left school at fourteen and went to work on the pig farm, unable to read and write; the transit camp Ophelia; the boy who wore dresses.

When the Everyman Theatre asked me to write a new play I began walking the city with my friend, the writer Lindsay Rodden, who became my dramaturg. Time and time again we were drawn to the ruins of the Futurist Cinema on Lime Street. I would tell Lindsay stories of my childhood, of my whole Terence Davies-hued love for palaces of dreams. I began to write about my feral characters, placing them in buildings like the Futurist. Character and place were one and the same, the ultimate dramatic unity. The people and the place would represent otherness, the wild city where foxes roam at night. I wanted to celebrate disobedience.

As Lizzie the firebrand says in the play: 'No one needs a dirty old fleapit full of snotty kids and weeping mums. They kind of wiped the Futurist off the Things to See and Do list. They let it die.'

Conveniently the building was falling to pieces. Its fate was written, but it wasn't going to give up without a fight. My characters seized the building and squatted in it, determined to bring it back to life, even as the dust fell on their heads.

All of this is key to my emotional – and philosophical – attachment to the city. If Liverpool didn't exist – and increasingly my personal vision of the city doesn't exist – then somebody would have to invent it. My characters proceeded to do so. The question they kept asking was, 'Who owns the City?' It certainly wasn't the people.

I remember watching certain films in the Futurist, even though I almost certainly watched them elsewhere. The first time I ever saw Powell and Pressburger's masterpiece, *A Matter of Life and Death*, it was most likely on television, but in my memory, I watched it in the Futurist. One of the first scenes I wrote in *Bright Phoenix* was the one where the gang bunk into the Futurist and act out the opening sequence in the film, in which David Niven, having crashed in his burning Lancaster bomber, falls in love with June, the beautiful radio operator. Blowing clouds of cigarette smoke, the kids laugh and swoon at the great romance of it all until they're thrown out by the usherette. Watching the flickering shadows of the film projected onto the walls of the Everyman, while the characters mimic the voices of Peter and June, was like gazing into a haunted space where cinematic magic, distorted memory and elegy for a lost building came together in a seance. It was the closest I could get to a resurrection ritual. I tried to make the play a song of praise to dissidence and disruption, to the liberating potential of the imagination.

I used to think of Lime Street as a place made from films. It had three cinemas, and the movies spilled out of them, flooded the street and animated the pavements with mystery, desire and drama. You could watch the street in the same way you'd watch a film. Over the years it became degraded, an increasingly negative space where the carnival of city life gave way to despair and ruin. When the cinemas closed down and the Scala became a lap-dancing club you could sense the vitality of the street turning to torpor. The rough edges that had always been there grew rougher. Instead of a street it became a gutter.

I grew to think of Lime Street as a fault line – a cultural and imaginative rift between magic and dreams on one side, and cynicism and greed on the other. In *Bright Phoenix*, the street ruptures, opens up like the sutures on a wound. In an early scene,

Spike the one-eyed derelict sees a vision of night-crawlers falling into the city's bowels: 'The city ripped the length of Lime Street. Buildings fell. Drunks, dogs, mad bastards, taxis full of hen nights, legless beggars ... fell between the cracks into the guts of Liverpool.'

Egged on by Spike, the gang maraud through the city at night, bringing the abandoned remnants of old buildings to the Futurist, intent on creating a Phoenix. They are utopian gleaners, making a new city out of the old.

As Spike says: 'Places are closing down all the time – community centres, boozers, libraries, swimming baths. And once a building's closed, it dies before your eyes. The roof caves in, cellars flood, windows smash. And they wait. They wait so long that people forget the building's there. Knock it down, done for.'

And later on, stirred up by the gang's magic ritual: '… the sound of car horns, taxi horns, bus horns comes in from the streets. They look at each other, smiling. And then a seismic shudder comes.

Pieces of the building fall. Dust drops. Beneath their feet – as if they are in an earthquake zone – the ground begins to rupture. A crack appears … Spike's apocalyptic vision is coming true.'

It's early 2019 and I'm on Lime Street with the film-maker John Maxwell. We've spent several hours mapping the street, filming, making sound recordings, taking photographs of the new development that's replaced the Futurist, the Scala and most of the neighbouring buildings. We stand on the street outside the supermarket where the Futurist used to be, trying to make sense of the monstrous banality of the new properties. The building looks like a cut-price kitchen unit, or some dubious type of packaging material, the sort that wraps a cheap fridge. The surfaces of the cladding look like they've been scrawled on by someone with a felt-tipped pen. According to the developer's website this frieze on the building's façade is intended to be:

> A Quantum Timeline, using illustrative graphic image and archived text to immortalise the development, buildings, business, people and heritage of Lime Street which was formerly known as Limekiln Lane. It will serve to forever mark and display what was as we celebrate what comes next. As one of the most important gateways to the city, we have an opportunity to reflect the vibrancy and history of the street in the elevations of the building – to offer a unique welcome to visitors who may not know anything of Liverpool, its fascinating narrative, and most importantly, its people.

Even though the development looks temporary – as if it's waiting for the home delivery men to schlep it to the right address – it will be here forever. It towers over the two pubs like a great big slab of nothing, a representation of imagination's death.

Bright Phoenix became an elegy for the Futurist – not long after the play was staged the cinema was demolished. On the spot where you can now buy dozens and dozens of crisp and chocolate brands, I once watched Disney cartoons, Beatles films, *Mary Poppins*, *The Wizard of Oz*, James Bond adventures, spaghetti westerns, *Mean*

Streets. I even watched a double bill of Andy Warhol's *Bad* and *Flesh for Frankenstein*, right there, in the Scala, next door to the Futurist where a gang of imagineers in a theatre play built a bright phoenix in the rubble and dust of a palace of dreams. In one sense they failed because the developers seized the territory; but in another sense they won because they imagined a better future. They enhanced the world with a beautiful idea. Things change, and change can be good. But change can also diminish. No one will ever again say that last night they went down Lime Street, unless in a story about buying a bumper pack of toilet rolls. No one will ever again stand beneath umbrellas in a queue to the matinee of *Love is a Many-Splendored Thing*.

The fox is walking down the street. It meets up with a skulk of other foxes out for a night of scavenging in the shadow-haunts of the city. Coming from somewhere above the chimney pots there is the sound of a voice, singing a song of anguish and desire. A pub singer – a phantom crooner – serenading the wounded city with a love song:

> We're all made of skin and bones
> And rights and wrongs
> And when the lights are turned down low
> We all dance to the same old songs.

In a crack in the cladding of the Lime Street development a buddleia is growing – a small shoot at first, but then bigger, stronger. The wild weed is returning to the new ruins of Liverpool and the tarmac is beginning to crack. Out of the gaps crawl feral men, wild women and beasts. I hear a howl. Listen to the street opera of Liverpool, to the feral song.

The night belongs to the fox.

Ghost Town

I am looking for a tree, the one that was twice as tall as my dad, the tree with a hole in its gut, like a belly button. It was just a bit higher than my head – a dark, mossy cavity where my sister Val hid a signet ring that she got from a bubblegum machine, deciding straightaway that this would be our hiding place, a place to keep our treasure. The Stanley Park treasure-tree was just around the corner from our house. Whenever we had some small change Val and I would spend it on the gum machines, and the hole in the tree became a magpie's nest of tiny squirt guns, a roulette wheel no bigger than a penny, a sheriff's badge, a magnifying glass. The machine outside Auntie Dot's corner shop on Goodison Road was the best source of treasure, and it was here that Val taught me how to scrape chewing gum off paving stones and get the last of the mint or juice out by pressing the hard disc between my tongue and the roof of my mouth. We got away with this most days until my mother caught me scraping a Juicy Fruit off the kerbstone and popping it between my teeth. My sister of course was away down the street, skipping a rope, and I was the one who got in trouble. Every time we went to Stanley Park we would check the tree and the treasure would still be there. We did this until the day we moved house, when we left the trinkets in the hollow and never went back. And now, fifty-five years later I'm looking for the tree, half hoping I'll put my hand inside the hollow and pull out a tiny penknife or a plastic toy soldier. But of course, the tree is no longer there.

It's a match day. Everton are playing Watford. Crowds of men and boys are walking through the park, heading to the ground. At 2.55pm the air-raid sirens begin to howl, psyching up the crowd, and then come the drums and pipes of 'Johnny Todd', and the roar and howl hurtles like an army of voices and I get that shiver down the spine I used to get when I was a kid, lying awake in bed when there was a night game, listening to the roaring noise like a battle above the chimney pots.

In my pocket, I have a tiny brass Buddha. It used to sit on Val's mantlepiece amongst all kinds of bric-a-brac and knick-knacks. The words FELICIDAD SUERTE SALUD are written on its base – happiness, luck and health. My plan had been to hide it inside the hollow tree as a way of completing the circle of a story. In truth, I don't think I'd have been able to leave it behind, but I liked the idea of a symbolic ritual, a secret ceremonial placing of a Buddha amongst a pile of bubblegum-machine treasure. The Buddha is a talisman; it connects me to my sister and this visit to the park is an attempt to shake off a bleak feeling of loss. Suddenly, a memory presents itself, summoned up by this spot on the footpath, of a snowball as big as Jupiter; dirty-grey and dog-piss yellow, taller than two dads, Val and I trying to push it down the pathway, laughing. And then at the boating lake I see our dog Dixie sliding on thin ice from one bank to another, howling as he goes, Val and I running, praying that the ice will hold, running through snow to the far bank to pull the dog to safety.

I leave the park and walk through the cemetery, down the slope where we used to play roly poly, past the broken angels in whose hands we used to place dead flowers. The war memorial is long and narrow, like a cricket pitch, the burial ground for three hundred unknown soldiers. My sister and I spent hours pressing acorns into the earth, hoping they would grow into oak trees, a long rectangular forest. Once, we filled a jam jar here with rain-wet acorns and beechnuts. In time the acorns sprouted roots, then rotted in the jar, as if they were fermenting. We used to fill our pockets with sycamore helicopters and the petals of plastic daffodils we found scattered between forgotten graves –the plastic flowers just like the ones that used to come free with Omo and Daz. I leave the cemetery and stop at the gates of Gwladys Street School, which looks exactly the same as it did in the 1960s. While Val was skipping a rope or playing two-balls, I was playing cops and robbers, biting a digestive biscuit into the shape of a hand gun.

I remember the day I took the wooden boat I got for Christmas into school for a show and tell. I was so proud of the yacht and I wanted to share it with the other children in my class. But the teacher laughed at me for bringing it in. I must have misunderstood the purpose of the exercise. Other children had brought in a book or a picture, and I had brought in something that made my teacher laugh at me, which made my classmates single me out as someone they could laugh at, too. I remember a boy carving my name into my desk and filling the cavity with ink. I remember being sent home with a letter saying I had to come to school with a Brillo pad and scouring powder. During playtime, I sat scrubbing the gouged hole, trying to get the inkstain out of the wood.

There is a photograph of me when I was maybe seven years old. I am a boy in black and white, my body white, my shorts black. I'm not wearing a shirt and I look as if I am shivering on that cold day on Central Beach in Prestatyn. My head is tilted to one side and I am smiling shyly, proudly. What am I proud of? I am proud of my toy boat. I hold it by the top of its mast, my right hand a loose fist enclosing the wooden rod, my left hand folding the sail between my fingers. I'm standing on the concrete steps leading down to the dull-grey mud-sand of our holiday beach in North Wales, the sand we play on every summer, the place I assume always was and always will be central to our universe. Once a year, Uncle Alf the butcher drives us in his posh Rover to his caravan on a farmer's field, where we spend our days caterpillar-hunting along the hedgerows, foraging for mushrooms and paddling in the murky Irish Sea. Sometimes we sit on a huge slate slab at the farm gate and watch the dairy men collecting milk churns. Every day we walk to the beach; sometimes we go on the pedal boats in the shabby amusement park; and every year on the third or fourth day of the holiday I get sunburn and have to go to bed early, smothered in ointments. I must have walked home from school, carrying the boat. I must have felt foolish and lonely.

I pass the church where we were christened and walk through the crowds of blue-topped fans. This is where my dad and I watched in horror as a police horse suddenly buckled under its own weight and collapsed in slow motion, pulling the policeman down with it, trapping him under its body. It went into convulsions, emitting masses of blood from its mouth, its body jerking as if it were having an epileptic seizure, and then it went quiet, becalmed in death. The memory burnt into me. And yet I didn't see it – my mother did. Presumably from hearing my mother tell the story – perhaps to a visitor when I was small – that terrible event had somehow passed into me and become my own memory. Once again, I am outside the house where we were born. I stand on the bubblegum pavement and look at the front door with an overwhelming feeling that this is home.

Seriously ill in hospital and close to the end of her life, Val told me she couldn't remember where she lived. She had no memory of home. She had been hallucinating in her hospital bed, living inside nightmares, imagining she was in prison or a train station, lost. But not being able to remember the house she'd lived in for over thirty years was different; it wasn't a hallucination, it was a frightening, bewildering loss. An entire house and its meanings had fallen out of her mind into oblivion. She could remember parts of the life she lived there with her husband and children, but she couldn't remember anything about the building itself – the bricks, mortar and glass, the furniture and ornaments, the architecture of home.

She thought perhaps it might have four stone steps leading to the front door, but this was not so. She thought it might be next to a rugby field, but this wasn't the case either.

When she came home from hospital she sat in her favourite armchair and I could see the fear in her eyes, in the darting glances around the room. And between each glance at an object she'd look to me and nervously smile, and nod and quietly say, 'Yes...' as if she were convincing herself that everything was in the right place. I wonder if was she seeing things as if for the first time and conducting an inventory, trying to memorise everything. I sometimes thought she didn't know who we were. She would cast a quizzical glance, trying to get the measure of us. I once saw her looking at me with such scrutiny that I felt the need to say to her, 'It's okay Val...it's me, Jeff...' And she would see things that weren't there – a bird coming out of the wallpaper, a child walking towards her, a shape she couldn't define looming out of the kitchen door. The house was being overtaken by her visions and I had a very real sense that death was in the shadows. My sister was frightened, but – hoping we wouldn't notice – she would laugh and say how lovely it was to be home.

We would tell stories and look at old photographs. Our favourite was a picture of a woman and two children in a dark room long ago. The woman is wearing a sleeveless dress patterned with squares that look like Jacob's Cream Crackers. Hair bobbed short, a smile of delight. This woman is our mother. Standing next to her is a small child in bib-and-brace dungarees and a knitted jumper. She gazes into the camera, short-haired, eyebrows arched, face a little grubby. She holds a red apple with two bites taken out of it, presenting it to the photographer – to us – as if to say, this is the proudest of apples, the reddest of fruits ... *and it's mine!* This child is my sister Val. Her right hand hangs loose at her side like a tiny gunslinger's trigger hand. Her left hand holds the apple, her fingers cupping the fruit, as if she is offering it to us, giving us a gift.

On mum's knee, there is a baby wearing a white dress and knitted cardigan, bald, fat-cheeked, bare feet. This baby is me. My mother's right hand looks so strong as it holds me upright. My right hand rests for security on her forearm, gently trusting. The room is gloomy, the chair has a lace-fringed antimacassar draped over the back, and it looks like the 1930s in this room, sort of poor but doing our best. It's actually the late 1950s, but in Liverpool when I was a child time seemed to have collapsed into a mangled heap. In the streets with their bomb sites it was post-Blitz dereliction. We look like people from a distant time. Presumably the dress I am wearing is a cast-off frock of my sister Val's. For a fleeting moment of intense clarity, I can hear my mother's laughter, out of the dust and shadow, the thing about her that everyone remembers, laughter like a bell.

The family sits in that dark room. I have hardly any memories of bright rooms. It's a house made of shadows, but the memories are full of light. The people in the photo are the lights. There is a photograph of my mum's sister, Margaret, sitting on the doorstep of the Winslow Street house. I wonder if this is the same day as the apple photograph? Margaret is smiling down at my sister Val, holding me on her lap. I am looking at my sister as she looks inside a bag. The doorway in the photo frames a deep black space, a rectangle of darkness, the interior of our house. This is the step where we used to wait for the rag-and-bone man, who would give us a balloon in exchange for some rags or scrap. Here comes the Prudential man in his fingerless gloves, beret and gabardine mac, propping his black bicycle on the front step, fingers wiping a bead of sweat from his military mustache. Here comes the Everton manager Harry Catterick presenting a bunch of flowers and 'the apologies of Everton F. C.' to my mum, heavily pregnant with my sister Kathryn, because she was woken from her afternoon nap by the boozed-up larking about of three of the team.

We watched The Beatles on the television in this house. I think it was the Royal Variety Performance in November 1963, when I

was six years old. Grandad Albert said, 'They'll do alright, those lads. They're from Liverpool,' and this struck us as a thrilling revelation. Sometimes when we walked through town we would look for them. On Mathew Street or in Brian Epstein's record shop we would look for Ringo Starr. We never saw him. Instead we often saw Ken Dodd and we would follow him around department stores looking at his hair. On a big fat reel-to-reel tape recorder we would record ourselves singing Dave Clark Five songs and The Beatles 'She Loves You', emphasis on the 'Yeah, Yeah, Yeahs', laughing when we played back the recording at the electronic distortion of our voices. *We were The Beatles*. The Future had arrived and we were in at its beginning. The buildings of Liverpool were black with soot in those days. I thought they were supposed to be that colour and that perhaps they were made of coal. Out of this darkness a new city grew. I thought it would be an experimental city. I had read about the space age in *Look and Learn* and every week I read *Dan Dare*, the *Eagle* comic hero and his interplanetary adventures. I watched *The Jetsons* on television, living their futuristic lives in Orbit City. Val and I would sit on the carpet in front of our Grundig television, lost in the supermarionated future of *Fireball XL5* and *Joe 90*.

There seemed to be a sense that the city was waking from a troubled sleep of trauma and decay into a bright new morning. Optimism was the new dawn's pep pill, an amphetamine boost of energy soundtracked by Fab Four harmonies and whoops. The buildings would no longer be soot-black; from now on they would be concrete-grey and look like multistorey car parks. When the vision was revealed to the waiting hordes it was a terrible disappointment. The flyovers were nothing more than a clumsy attempt to manage traffic jams. The aerial walkways were never completed, there would never be Sci-Fi pavements in the sky. In truth, the ventilation shaft on North John Street – another breathtaking masterpiece designed by Herbert J. Rowse – was more futuristic than these bleak 1960s interventions; sheer as an Art Deco cliff face fit for peregrines, a slipstreamed Pegasus imprinted on its top right-hand corner. This was the visionary future dreamed by poet-architects and stone masons. Even as a child I was aware that the city was being *imaginatively reduced.*

As the St John's Precinct beacon rose above the streets, I was hoping it would be a space station spinning across a new Liverpool – perhaps a city drawn by Frank Hampson, the man who dreamed Dan Dare. The reality was that the beacon was a 452-feet chimney for the shopping centre's waste incinerator. Sometimes we would go up the tower for a knickerbocker glory, thrilling to the high-speed, thirty-second journey to the top, then eating our disappointing ices with long spoons in a slowly revolving café like a Little Chef in the sky. A suitable soundtrack might have been The Tornadoes playing 'Telstar'. Instead we had to listen to James Last's 'Trumpet A Go Go, Volume 2'. But up on the viewing platform you could see forever. There we stood, in our duffel coats, after going to the grotto in Blacklers, watching the sundae sunset slowly melting into the sea.

I go to the Everton water tower and look at its demonic ghost-face peering over the rooftops. On those Sundays when we used to go to nana and grandad's house in Grey Rock Street, I was fascinated by the water tower. You could see it in the distance and it would scare me a little as it peeped over falling-down buildings. I used to think that Brunel had built it, but the architect was Thomas Duncan, Liverpool's first water engineer. With its arched arcades, it looks like the Colosseum. Once it was a reservoir, now it stands empty. It used to see everything. It was a witness. It looks lonely amongst the semi-detached houses. It looks blind.

Not far from here, my great-grandad Michael spent part of his childhood in the Everton poorhouse, in what used to be called the Industrial – or 'Ragged' – School, going in at the age of thirteen and leaving when he was fifteen. Boys like him were incarcerated for committing minor crimes, or thought to be in danger of doing so. Perhaps Michael's parents, who came from

Dublin in the 1860s, couldn't cope with his behaviour. But while he was inside he learnt to mend shoes, and when he came out he set himself up in business as a cobbler. My dad said he turned the front parlour of his house into a shop by knocking the front wall out. He mended shoes for the rest of his life.

There are no photographs of great-grandad Michael. I don't know what he looked like. If photographs are a conduit into memory – a way of fixing an image of someone, and a way of staging a setting for that memory to be acted out – how do I conjure up an image of this great-grandparent when no photographs exist? He was twelve years dead by the time I was born, and yet I have images in my mind, like a flickering cinema, of him moving through his parlour. I can see him, hobnails between his teeth, hammering away at the leather soles of boots in his workshop. I can see his face, looking at me down the years, even if I don't actually know what his face looked like. I fill the empty space with an invented memory. As I wander through the city I realise I am feeling a kind of spiritual loss. My connection with the city I have loved all my life has become frayed. I go looking for the Ragged School, but it's long gone, and no one walking down the street is aware it was ever even there.

Across the road from the poor house site is the Locarno where circus elephants and lions once lived in cages in the basement and trapeze artists flew above the heads of my grandparents, Emma and Jim. I am sitting in the Locarno – now called the Olympia – with Amy and Pearl. On stage, Nick Cave is singing Marc Bolan's beautiful 'Cosmic Dancer' during an evening in which he talks of death, God and love. I sit looking at plaster casts of elephant heads, seeking in the shabby darkness Emma's and Jim's ghosts. In the early 1900s, in this beautiful Frank Matcham theatre, in scenes that might have been written by Angela Carter, 'aquatic displays' of great sea battles were enacted in a pit flooded with 80,000 gallons of water. Circus seals performed tricks to excited children. Harry Houdini was smuggled like a pop star through secret tunnels running beneath the road to the safety of the Olympia hotel. Not far from here is the site where my dad looted the air-raid shelters after the Second World War had ended, a teenage ne'er-do-well stripping the cellars of beds and flogging the timber for firewood.

I go to a place in the past that once seemed like the future – to the bucket fountain on Beetham Plaza where we first came in the week it opened in 1967. Richard Huws' kinetic sculpture is a mechanical theatre where water overflows from pivoted metal tanks in an endless cycle of tilting, emptying out and gradual refilling. The noise of the water gushing from the buckets, down into the pool below and then gurgling back up to the buckets brings the sound of waterfalls into the city. It is a thing of joy, an amusing intervention in the city's business district. When we were young it was one of the stopping-off places on those days when Liverpool was our very own amusement park. Standing there, remembering how we used to try and guess which bucket would be 'the next tipper', I get talking to a woman who tells me developers are planning to move the buckets to another part of the city to make way for a hotel. I tell her I used to play here with my sister. *'I'm just reminiscing...'*. In reality, even though we came here over and over again, I am struggling to remember the details of those visits, but the familiarity of the clank of metal and the whoosh of water echoing against the office blocks *feel* like memory, imbues the moment with nostalgia. And then I can see us – small children in 1967, laughing at this magical contraption.

So many places and people are disappearing. The bucket fountain is what gives this place meaning; if they remove this mad and beautiful machine there will be no reason to ever visit this city square again. *Strangeness, eccentricity, secrecy and wonder are constantly being erased...*

At the age of sixty-four, my sister Val was diagnosed with not one, but two terminal diseases and came home from hospital to end her life. This was the home where she brought up her children, Mathew, Daniel and Emma, where she told her famously exaggerated stories, where she recovered from breast cancer, where her husband Phil died when she was forty-two, where she made everyone laugh along with her own laughter, a kind of joy against the odds in an often difficult life. The house is an echo-chamber. It does what I spend my life doing – it remembers. It is memory itself.

A few days before she died we made her a garden, filling her backyard with geraniums, petunias, lavender and even wild Welsh poppies that we uprooted from the garden of the empty house next door. Fat Buddhas, garden gnomes, pottery ducks and owls took their place amongst the flowers, and when we had finished we opened the curtains so Val could see the transformed yard through the window next to her bed. She would never get to sit in her garden, but it made her smile. Two days later she was dead.

On the morning after her death, I wander around her house looking at her possessions. Objects cover every surface, holiday souvenirs and mementoes, gifts and charity-shop finds, car-boot-sale novelties. None of these things has monetary worth, but because Val has invested every object with meaning and memory the value is immense. The objects and photographs seem to speak. They tell stories of holidays in Spain and ice creams in Prestatyn. There are souvenirs inscribed with homilies and mottos: *Life isn't about waiting for the storm to pass. It's about learning to dance in the rain; Peace be to this house and to all who dwell in it. Peace to them that enter and to them that depart.* There are Portuguese 'Rooster of Barcelos' ornaments, elephants, top-hatted dogs, glass swans, Buddhas, owls, dolphins, angel fish. Val's house is a cabinet of curiosities, an exhibition, an autobiography. In her bedroom, we find a holdall full of bracelets, necklaces, brooches and earrings, enough to make you wonder if she'd been a jewel thief. There are so many pairs of glasses she could have opened her own opticians. And there are dozens and dozens of pairs of shoes. She created a glass menagerie of elephants and dogs. She never stopped collecting treasure. In a sense, she had always been a magpie, collecting bubblegum-machine trinkets and hiding them in the hollow of a tree.

And when, a few weeks after her death, things were packed into boxes and her son Mathew stripped away the wallpaper and plaster, exposing the bricks, it was as if she had disappeared into the walls, had been subsumed into the dead-insect and cobwebby dust and crumbling mortar. My sister no longer physically existed in the house in which she died but she was somehow still there. It was as if she had become the house, and the house had become her.

Determined not to submit to amnesia, the house makes a decision not to forget...

As I walk out of this memory place, I feel overwhelmed with exhaustion and a kind of nausea. I don't want to do this anymore. Whatever it is I'm looking for, whatever it is I'm trying to resolve, all of it seems futile. And then it occurs to me that without all this churning anxiety and remembering I do not exist. Walking along the canal towpath back into town, I remember Val and I coming to the cut with jam jars to catch sticklebacks, dipping our fishing nets into the canal's dark waters. We didn't know that tap water would kill them, and so we filled our jars with dozens of silvery green fish, glinting in the sunlight like tiny brooches, took them home and poured them into a tankful of tap water where they quickly died. Just like the sticklebacks, the memories are glinting.

Liverpool is the haunted place of remembering. I walk through the city and suddenly a new memory presents itself of me closing my sister's eyes, seconds after she died, my fingertip wet with a teardrop. There are faces in the shadows of old buildings. There are voices singing songs. I follow the sound down back streets and into the glorious sunset. I'm doing what I always do. I am looking for my ghosts.

Acknowledgements

Parts of this book were originally broadcast on radio in slightly different form. 'Transformer' was featured in BBC Radio 3's *In the Shadow of Kafka* season in 2014. 'Gutted Arcades', 'Glass Constellations'' and 'Haunted Lullaby' were part of the five-episode Essay series, *Kaleidoscope of Muses* broadcast on BBC Radio 3 in 2018. All of these pieces were produced by Polly Thomas and Eloise Whitmore, thanks as ever to them and to Mathew Dodd at Radio 3 for commissioning me. Parts of 'Grandfather, Grey Rock' were published by Capsicum Books in 2007 in slightly different form in their 'Liverpool Longing', thanks to Deborah Mulhearn. The radio dramas 'The Hunt for Billy Casper' and 'Red Rock, Grey Rock' mentioned in the book were brilliantly produced and directed by Mel Harris for BBC Radio 3 and 4. The theatre play 'Bright Phoenix' was commissioned and produced by the Liverpool Everyman Theatre and directed by Serdar Billis. Thanks to Serdar and Gemma Bodinetz, to Bloomsbury books for publishing it, and to all the Bright Phoenix company, especially Lindsay Rodden and Martin Heslop. It was the best of times. Thanks to Matt and Alex at Berlin Associates and Sarah Maclennan and the team at Liverpool John Moores University Screen School. I'm grateful to Adrian, Gracie, Graham and Jon at Little Toller for their incredible support and patience through a rather troubled year.

Love and thanks to Horatio Clare who walked with me and pointed me in the direction of Little Toller. To the Wild Swan Paul Simpson for friendship, inspiration and Wednesday afternoons in the Little Grapes. David Lewis for haunting the city with me for over thirty years. Peter O'Halligan for the dream. John Buscombe for just about everything. Jill Heslop for friendship and collaboration on the 'Jeff's Brain' installation, which was the root of so many of these musings. Thanks to Alan Dunn, Demelza Kooij, Richard Monks and Jo Pocock for all the inspiring talking and walking through this city, and to Anna Maria Murphy for the Kneehigh Liverpool Rambles. Hats off to Shaun and Jen at Metal, Edge Hill and John Maxwell for our shared fantasy of a new Futurist cinema rising from the ruins. Every time I walk through this city I look for my spirit of place, Frank Miles, the greatest storyteller I ever met, may he rest in peace. And I'd like to send a signal to the lost boys and girls of childhood wherever they may be.

Love to the families Young, Hampson, Petricca and Buscombe, especially my sister Kathryn, Auntie Margaret and my dad Cyril. The most important people to thank are my beloved Amy and our daughter Pearl for all their amazing love, patience and laughter. I love you very much.

Finally this book is dedicated to the memory of my mum, Maureen Young and to my beautiful sister Val, one of the muses of this book who sadly died during the writing of it. Love to you both. The world will never be the same again. *Where did you go? And why are you not here?*

J. Y., Liverpool, 2020

Little Toller Books

FORD, PINEAPPLE LANE, DORSET
w. littletoller.co.uk   e. books@littletoller.co.uk